"After utilizing toolkits from The Art of Service, I was able to identify threats within my organization to which I was completely unaware. Using my team's knowledge as a competitive advantage, we now have superior systems that save time and energy."

"As a new Chief Technology Officer, I was feeling unprepared and inadequate to be successful in my role. I ordered an IT toolkit Sunday night and was prepared Monday morning to shed light on areas of improvement within my organization. I no longer felt overwhelmed and intimidated, I was excited to share what I had learned."

"I used the questionnaires to interview members of my team. I never knew how many insights we could produce collectively with our internal knowledge."

"I usually work until at least 8pm on weeknights. The Art of Service questionnaire saved me so much time and worry that Thursday night I attended my son's soccer game without sacrificing my professional obligations."

"After purchasing The Art of Service toolkit, I was able to identify areas where my company was not in compliance that could have put my job at risk. I looked like a hero when I proactively educated my team on the risks and presented a solid solution."

"I spent months shopping for an external consultant before realizing that The Art of Service would allow my team to consult themselves! Not only did we save time not catching a consultant up to speed, we were able to keep our company information and industry secrets confidential."

"Everyday there are new regulations and processes in my industry. The Art of Service toolkit has kept me ahead by using AI technology to constantly update the toolkits and address emerging needs."

"I customized The Art of Service toolkit to focus specifically on the concerns of my role and industry. I didn't have to waste time with a generic self-help book that wasn't tailored to my exact situation."

"Many of our competitors have asked us about our secret sauce. When I tell them it's the knowledge we have in-house, they never believe me. Little do they know The Art of Service toolkits are working behind the scenes."

"One of my friends hired a consultant who used the knowledge gained working with his company to advise their competitor. Talk about a competitive disadvantage! The Art of Service allowed us to keep our knowledge from walking out the door along with a huge portion of our budget in consulting fees."

"Honestly, I didn't know what I didn't know. Before purchasing The Art of Service, I didn't realize how many areas of my business needed to be refreshed and improved. I am so relieved The Art of Service was there to highlight our blind spots."

"Before The Art of Service, I waited eagerly for consulting company reports to come out each month. These reports kept us up to speed but provided little value because they put our competitors on the same playing field. With The Art of Service, we have uncovered unique insights to drive our business forward."

"Instead of investing extensive resources into an external consultant, we can spend more of our budget towards pursuing our company goals and objectives…while also spending a little more on corporate holiday parties."

"The risk of our competitors getting ahead has been mitigated because The Art of Service has provided us with a 360-degree view of threats within our organization before they even arise."

CCNP
Complete Self-Assessment Guide

Table of Contents

About The Art of Service

The Art of Service, Business Process Architects since 2000, is dedicated to helping stakeholders achieve excellence.

Defining, designing, creating, and implementing a process to solve a stakeholders challenge or meet an objective is the most valuable role… In EVERY group, company, organization and department.

Unless you're talking a one-time, single-use project, there should be a process. Whether that process is managed and implemented by humans, AI, or a combination of the two, it needs to be designed by someone with a complex enough perspective to ask the right questions.

Someone capable of asking the right questions and step back and say, 'What are we really trying to accomplish here? And is there a different way to look at it?'

With The Art of Service's Self-Assessments, we empower people who can do just that — whether their title is marketer, entrepreneur, manager, salesperson, consultant, Business Process Manager, executive assistant, IT Manager, CIO etc... —they are the people who rule the future. They are people who watch the process as it happens, and ask the right questions to make the process work better.

Contact us when you need any support with this Self-Assessment and any help with templates, blue-prints and examples of standard documents you might need:

https://theartofservice.com
support@theartofservice.com

Included Resources - how to access

Included with your purchase of the book is the CCNP Self-

Assessment Spreadsheet Dashboard which contains all questions and Self-Assessment areas and auto-generates insights, graphs, and project RACI planning - all with examples to get you started right away.

How? Simply send an email to
access@theartofservice.com
with this books' title in the subject to get the CCNP Self Assessment Tool right away.

The auto reply will guide you further, you will then receive the following contents with New and Updated specific criteria:

- The latest quick edition of the book in PDF

- The latest complete edition of the book in PDF, which criteria correspond to the criteria in...

- The Self-Assessment Excel Dashboard, and...

- Example pre-filled Self-Assessment Excel Dashboard to get familiar with results generation

- In-depth specific Checklists covering the topic

- Project management checklists and templates to assist with implementation

INCLUDES LIFETIME SELF ASSESSMENT UPDATES

Every self assessment comes with Lifetime Updates and Lifetime Free Updated Books. Lifetime Updates is an industry-first feature which allows you to receive verified self assessment updates, ensuring you always have the most accurate information at your fingertips.

Get it now- you will be glad you did - do it now, before you forget.

Send an email to **access@theartofservice.com** with this books' title in the subject to get the CCNP Self Assessment Tool right away.

Purpose of this Self-Assessment

This Self-Assessment has been developed to improve understanding of the requirements and elements of CCNP, based on best practices and standards in business process architecture, design and quality management.

It is designed to allow for a rapid Self-Assessment to determine how closely existing management practices and procedures correspond to the elements of the Self-Assessment.

The criteria of requirements and elements of CCNP have been rephrased in the format of a Self-Assessment questionnaire, with a seven-criterion scoring system, as explained in this document.

In this format, even with limited background knowledge of CCNP, a manager can quickly review existing operations to determine how they measure up to the standards. This in turn can serve as the starting point of a 'gap analysis' to identify management tools or system elements that might usefully be implemented in the organization to help improve overall performance.

How to use the Self-Assessment

On the following pages are a series of questions to identify to what extent your CCNP initiative is complete in comparison to the requirements set in standards.

To facilitate answering the questions, there is a space in front of each question to enter a score on a scale of '1' to '5'.

1 Strongly Disagree

2 Disagree

3 Neutral

4 Agree

5 Strongly Agree

Read the question and rate it with the following in front of mind:

'In my belief,
the answer to this question is clearly defined'.

There are two ways in which you can choose to interpret this statement;
1. how aware are you that the answer to the question is clearly defined
2. for more in-depth analysis you can choose to gather evidence and confirm the answer to the question. This obviously will take more time, most Self-Assessment users opt for the first way to interpret the question and dig deeper later on based on the outcome of the overall Self-Assessment.

A score of '1' would mean that the answer is not clear at all, where a '5' would mean the answer is crystal clear and defined. Leave emtpy when the question is not applicable or you don't want to answer it, you can skip it without affecting your score. Write your score in the space provided.

After you have responded to all the appropriate statements in each section, compute your average score for that section, using the formula provided, and round to the nearest tenth. Then transfer to the corresponding spoke in the CCNP Scorecard on the second next page of the Self-Assessment.

Your completed CCNP Scorecard will give you a clear presentation of which CCNP areas need attention.

CCNP
Scorecard Example

Example of how the finalized Scorecard can look like:

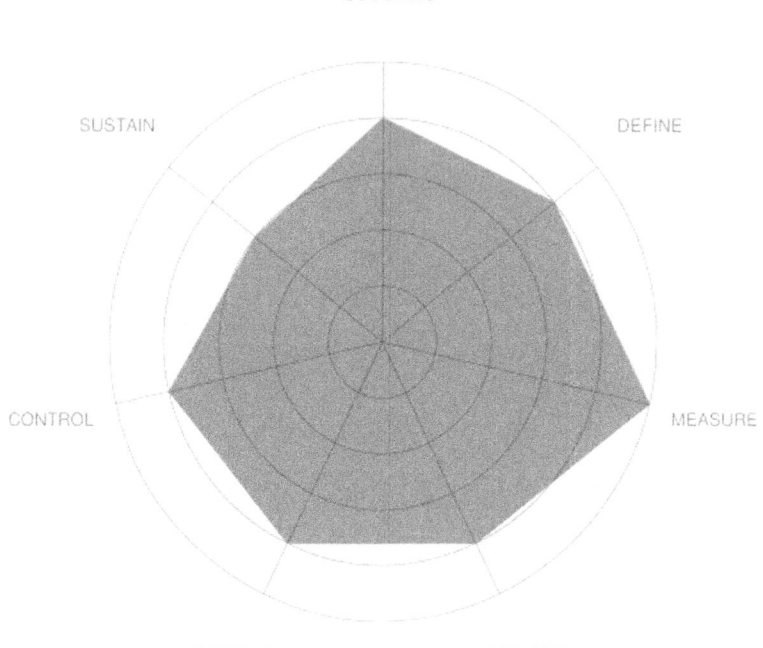

CCNP
Scorecard

Your Scores:

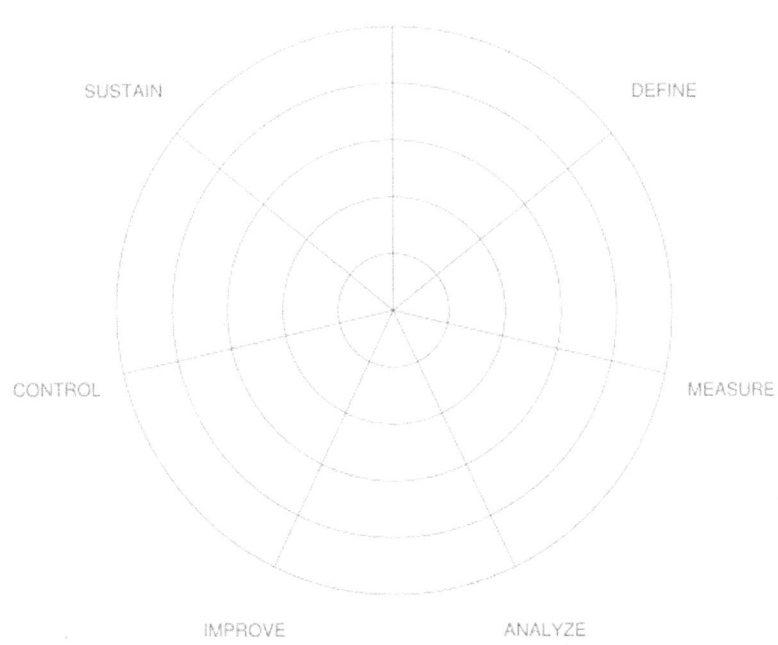

BEGINNING OF THE SELF-ASSESSMENT:

CRITERION #1: RECOGNIZE

INTENT: Be aware of the need for change. Recognize that there is an unfavorable variation, problem or symptom.

In my belief, the answer to this question is clearly defined:

5 Strongly Agree

4 Agree

3 Neutral

2 Disagree

1 Strongly Disagree

1. For your CCNP project, identify and describe the business environment, is there more than one layer to the business environment?
<--- Score

2. Which should be the first step in correcting problems at the network layer?
<--- Score

3. Looking at each person individually – does every one have the qualities which are needed to work in this group?
<--- Score

4. Which needs are not included or involved?
<--- Score

5. What CCNP capabilities do you need?
<--- Score

6. What is the extent or complexity of the CCNP problem?
<--- Score

7. Would you recognize a threat from the inside?
<--- Score

8. What information do users need?
<--- Score

9. Will new equipment/products be required to facilitate CCNP delivery, for example is new software needed?
<--- Score

10. How do you identify subcontractor relationships?
<--- Score

11. What are the CCNP resources needed?
<--- Score

12. Are there any specific expectations or concerns about the CCNP team, CCNP itself?
<--- Score

13. Who defines the rules in relation to any given issue?

<--- Score

14. Are there CCNP problems defined?

<--- Score

15. Is it possible to have network layer problems while the addresses are correct and routing is operational and functional?

<--- Score

16. What situation(s) led to this CCNP Self Assessment?

<--- Score

17. What do employees need in the short term?

<--- Score

18. What is the problem or issue?

<--- Score

19. Why is this needed?

<--- Score

20. What resources or support might you need?

<--- Score

21. What tools and technologies are needed for a custom CCNP project?

<--- Score

22. How many trainings, in total, are needed?

<--- Score

23. What else needs to be measured?

<--- Score

24. Which troubleshooting approach is most appropriate to implement if the problem is located at the network interface?
<--- Score

25. What does CCNP success mean to the stakeholders?
<--- Score

26. Did you miss any major CCNP issues?
<--- Score

27. Consider your own CCNP project, what types of organizational problems do you think might be causing or affecting your problem, based on the work done so far?
<--- Score

28. How are training requirements identified?
<--- Score

29. Are your goals realistic? Do you need to redefine your problem? Perhaps the problem has changed or maybe you have reached your goal and need to set a new one?
<--- Score

30. Which issues are too important to ignore?
<--- Score

31. Think about the people you identified for your CCNP project and the project responsibilities you would assign to them, what kind of training do you think they would need to perform these

responsibilities effectively?
<--- Score

32. Are controls defined to recognize and contain problems?
<--- Score

33. When a CCNP manager recognizes a problem, what options are available?
<--- Score

34. Does the problem have ethical dimensions?
<--- Score

35. Are there any revenue recognition issues?
<--- Score

36. Who should resolve the CCNP issues?
<--- Score

37. Are employees recognized or rewarded for performance that demonstrates the highest levels of integrity?
<--- Score

38. Why the need?
<--- Score

39. What prevents you from making the changes you know will make you a more effective CCNP leader?
<--- Score

40. Which guideline for isolating problems at the network layer should you practice next?
<--- Score

41. Are you dealing with any of the same issues today as yesterday? What can you do about this?
<--- Score

42. Do you need to avoid or amend any CCNP activities?
<--- Score

43. Have you identified your CCNP key performance indicators?
<--- Score

44. Who else hopes to benefit from it?
<--- Score

45. Who are your key stakeholders who need to sign off?
<--- Score

46. What are the stakeholder objectives to be achieved with CCNP?
<--- Score

47. Who needs to know about CCNP?
<--- Score

48. Where is training needed?
<--- Score

49. Who needs budgets?
<--- Score

50. Are there regulatory / compliance issues?
<--- Score

51. How does it fit into your organizational needs and

tasks?
<--- Score

52. How do you identify the kinds of information that you will need?
<--- Score

53. What is the problem and/or vulnerability?
<--- Score

54. As a sponsor, customer or management, how important is it to meet goals, objectives?
<--- Score

55. What CCNP events should you attend?
<--- Score

56. Can management personnel recognize the monetary benefit of CCNP?
<--- Score

57. Do you recognize CCNP achievements?
<--- Score

58. What is the smallest subset of the problem you can usefully solve?
<--- Score

59. Is the need for organizational change recognized?
<--- Score

60. Are employees recognized for desired behaviors?
<--- Score

61. How are you going to measure success?
<--- Score

62. Is the quality assurance team identified?
<--- Score

63. Is it clear when you think of the day ahead of you what activities and tasks you need to complete?
<--- Score

64. What CCNP problem should be solved?
<--- Score

65. Does CCNP create potential expectations in other areas that need to be recognized and considered?
<--- Score

66. What CCNP coordination do you need?
<--- Score

67. What are the minority interests and what amount of minority interests can be recognized?
<--- Score

68. What are the clients issues and concerns?
<--- Score

69. Will a response program recognize when a crisis occurs and provide some level of response?
<--- Score

70. Do you have/need 24-hour access to key personnel?
<--- Score

71. What vendors make products that address the CCNP needs?
<--- Score

72. Are there recognized CCNP problems?
<--- Score

73. What are the expected benefits of CCNP to the stakeholder?
<--- Score

74. What is the CCNP problem definition? What do you need to resolve?
<--- Score

75. Does your organization need more CCNP education?
<--- Score

76. What are your needs in relation to CCNP skills, labor, equipment, and markets?
<--- Score

77. How can auditing be a preventative security measure?
<--- Score

78. Which step of the recommended procedure for correcting problems at the network layer are you performing?
<--- Score

79. How do you recognize an objection?
<--- Score

80. Who needs what information?
<--- Score

81. Will CCNP deliverables need to be tested and, if so,

by whom?
<--- Score

82. How much are sponsors, customers, partners, stakeholders involved in CCNP? In other words, what are the risks, if CCNP does not deliver successfully?
<--- Score

83. What extra resources will you need?
<--- Score

84. Are losses recognized in a timely manner?
<--- Score

85. What problems are you facing and how do you consider CCNP will circumvent those obstacles?
<--- Score

86. What would happen if CCNP weren't done?
<--- Score

87. What creative shifts do you need to take?
<--- Score

88. How are the CCNP's objectives aligned to the group's overall stakeholder strategy?
<--- Score

89. What activities does the governance board need to consider?
<--- Score

90. How do you take a forward-looking perspective in identifying CCNP research related to market response and models?
<--- Score

91. Do you know what you need to know about CCNP?
<--- Score

92. What needs to stay?
<--- Score

93. What do you need to start doing?
<--- Score

94. Are problem definition and motivation clearly presented?
<--- Score

95. Whom do you really need or want to serve?
<--- Score

96. Who needs to know?
<--- Score

97. How do you recognize an CCNP objection?
<--- Score

98. Is it needed?
<--- Score

Add up total points for this section:

_ _ _ _ _ = Total points for this section

Divided by: _ _ _ _ _ _ (number of statements answered) = _ _ _ _ _ _
Average score for this section

Transfer your score to the CCNP Index at the beginning of the Self-Assessment.

CRITERION #2: DEFINE:

INTENT: Formulate the stakeholder problem. Define the problem, needs and objectives.

In my belief, the answer to this question is clearly defined:

5 Strongly Agree

4 Agree

3 Neutral

2 Disagree

1 Strongly Disagree

1. How does the CCNP manager ensure against scope creep?
<--- Score

2. What system do you use for gathering CCNP information?
<--- Score

3. What scope do you want your strategy to cover?

<--- Score

4. Are roles and responsibilities formally defined?
<--- Score

5. Who defines (or who defined) the rules and roles?
<--- Score

6. Have all basic functions of CCNP been defined?
<--- Score

7. Is there a critical path to deliver CCNP results?
<--- Score

8. How do you catch CCNP definition inconsistencies?
<--- Score

9. What is the definition of success?
<--- Score

10. Are there any constraints known that bear on the ability to perform CCNP work? How is the team addressing them?
<--- Score

11. How do you hand over CCNP context?
<--- Score

12. What are (control) requirements for CCNP Information?
<--- Score

13. Are different versions of process maps needed to account for the different types of inputs?
<--- Score

14. Is the current 'as is' process being followed? If not, what are the discrepancies?
<--- Score

15. What are the CCNP use cases?
<--- Score

16. Are audit criteria, scope, frequency and methods defined?
<--- Score

17. Is it clearly defined in and to your organization what you do?
<--- Score

18. How are consistent CCNP definitions important?
<--- Score

19. What defines best in class?
<--- Score

20. What is the definition of CCNP excellence?
<--- Score

21. If substitutes have been appointed, have they been briefed on the CCNP goals and received regular communications as to the progress to date?
<--- Score

22. How do you gather requirements?
<--- Score

23. When is/was the CCNP start date?
<--- Score

24. Is special CCNP user knowledge required?

<--- Score

25. What information should you gather?
<--- Score

26. What is the context?
<--- Score

27. What key stakeholder process output measure(s) does CCNP leverage and how?
<--- Score

28. Is there regularly 100% attendance at the team meetings? If not, have appointed substitutes attended to preserve cross-functionality and full representation?
<--- Score

29. Has anyone else (internal or external to the group) attempted to solve this problem or a similar one before? If so, what knowledge can be leveraged from these previous efforts?
<--- Score

30. How did the CCNP manager receive input to the development of a CCNP improvement plan and the estimated completion dates/times of each activity?
<--- Score

31. What critical content must be communicated – who, what, when, where, and how?
<--- Score

32. What CCNP requirements should be gathered?
<--- Score

33. Have the customer needs been translated into specific, measurable requirements? How?
<--- Score

34. Is the CCNP scope complete and appropriately sized?
<--- Score

35. How often are the team meetings?
<--- Score

36. Who are the CCNP improvement team members, including Management Leads and Coaches?
<--- Score

37. What are the boundaries of the scope? What is in bounds and what is not? What is the start point? What is the stop point?
<--- Score

38. What are the CCNP tasks and definitions?
<--- Score

39. Are accountability and ownership for CCNP clearly defined?
<--- Score

40. Is CCNP currently on schedule according to the plan?
<--- Score

41. How have you defined all CCNP requirements first?
<--- Score

42. What is the scope of CCNP?
<--- Score

43. Are the CCNP requirements testable?
<--- Score

44. Do you mix and match the current exams with newer exams to achieve CCNP Security?
<--- Score

45. Are there any requirements for food vendors to ensure food safety?
<--- Score

46. Are all requirements met?
<--- Score

47. Will a CCNP production readiness review be required?
<--- Score

48. Has your scope been defined?
<--- Score

49. Have specific policy objectives been defined?
<--- Score

50. What are the recertification requirements for CCNP Security?
<--- Score

51. Are task requirements clearly defined?
<--- Score

52. How do you gather CCNP requirements?
<--- Score

53. How do you think the partners involved in CCNP

would have defined success?
<--- Score

54. What are the Roles and Responsibilities for each team member and its leadership? Where is this documented?
<--- Score

55. What constraints exist that might impact the team?
<--- Score

56. How do you manage unclear CCNP requirements?
<--- Score

57. Are required metrics defined, what are they?
<--- Score

58. Has everyone on the team, including the team leaders, been properly trained?
<--- Score

59. Has a project plan, Gantt chart, or similar been developed/completed?
<--- Score

60. How do you manage changes in CCNP requirements?
<--- Score

61. How is the team tracking and documenting its work?
<--- Score

62. Why are you doing CCNP and what is the scope?
<--- Score

63. Has/have the customer(s) been identified?
<--- Score

64. What specifically is the problem? Where does it occur? When does it occur? What is its extent?
<--- Score

65. How was the 'as is' process map developed, reviewed, verified and validated?
<--- Score

66. What sort of initial information to gather?
<--- Score

67. Has a high-level 'as is' process map been completed, verified and validated?
<--- Score

68. What are the compelling stakeholder reasons for embarking on CCNP?
<--- Score

69. The political context: who holds power?
<--- Score

70. When are meeting minutes sent out? Who is on the distribution list?
<--- Score

71. Do you have organizational privacy requirements?
<--- Score

72. How do you build the right business case?
<--- Score

73. What sources do you use to gather information for a CCNP study?
<--- Score

74. What baselines are required to be defined and managed?
<--- Score

75. What scope to assess?
<--- Score

76. What was the context?
<--- Score

77. Has a CCNP requirement not been met?
<--- Score

78. What happens if CCNP's scope changes?
<--- Score

79. How do you gather the stories?
<--- Score

80. Has the improvement team collected the 'voice of the customer' (obtained feedback – qualitative and quantitative)?
<--- Score

81. What are the new prices of the Cisco CCNA and CCNP Composite exams?
<--- Score

82. Who is gathering CCNP information?
<--- Score

83. Is CCNP required?

<--- Score

84. Are approval levels defined for contracts and supplements to contracts?
<--- Score

85. What is the worst case scenario?
<--- Score

86. How will variation in the actual durations of each activity be dealt with to ensure that the expected CCNP results are met?
<--- Score

87. Who is gathering information?
<--- Score

88. What are the record-keeping requirements of CCNP activities?
<--- Score

89. How would you define the culture at your organization, how susceptible is it to CCNP changes?
<--- Score

90. What gets examined?
<--- Score

91. What would be the goal or target for a CCNP's improvement team?
<--- Score

92. How will the CCNP team and the group measure complete success of CCNP?
<--- Score

93. What is out-of-scope initially?
<--- Score

94. What information do you gather?
<--- Score

95. Is the team adequately staffed with the desired cross-functionality? If not, what additional resources are available to the team?
<--- Score

96. Is scope creep really all bad news?
<--- Score

97. What are the tasks and definitions?
<--- Score

98. Does the team have regular meetings?
<--- Score

99. Has a team charter been developed and communicated?
<--- Score

100. Is there a clear CCNP case definition?
<--- Score

101. Do you have a CCNP success story or case study ready to tell and share?
<--- Score

102. In what way can you redefine the criteria of choice clients have in your category in your favor?
<--- Score

103. Is the CCNP scope manageable?

<--- Score

104. Do the problem and goal statements meet the SMART criteria (specific, measurable, attainable, relevant, and time-bound)?
<--- Score

105. What intelligence can you gather?
<--- Score

106. When is the estimated completion date?
<--- Score

107. Are there different segments of customers?
<--- Score

108. What is a worst-case scenario for losses?
<--- Score

109. What knowledge or experience is required?
<--- Score

110. Where can you gather more information?
<--- Score

111. What CCNP services do you require?
<--- Score

112. Is there any additional CCNP definition of success?
<--- Score

113. What is in the scope and what is not in scope?
<--- Score

114. Have all of the relationships been defined

properly?
<--- Score

115. Is there a completed SIPOC representation, describing the Suppliers, Inputs, Process, Outputs, and Customers?
<--- Score

116. Is the improvement team aware of the different versions of a process: what they think it is vs. what it actually is vs. what it should be vs. what it could be?
<--- Score

117. Is CCNP linked to key stakeholder goals and objectives?
<--- Score

118. Is the work to date meeting requirements?
<--- Score

119. How do you manage scope?
<--- Score

120. Has the CCNP work been fairly and/or equitably divided and delegated among team members who are qualified and capable to perform the work? Has everyone contributed?
<--- Score

121. What are the requirements for audit information?
<--- Score

122. Who approved the CCNP scope?
<--- Score

123. Has the direction changed at all during the

course of CCNP? If so, when did it change and why?
<--- Score

124. Does the scope remain the same?
<--- Score

125. What are the dynamics of the communication plan?
<--- Score

126. Are the CCNP requirements complete?
<--- Score

127. What customer feedback methods were used to solicit their input?
<--- Score

128. What is the scope of the CCNP work?
<--- Score

129. How do you keep key subject matter experts in the loop?
<--- Score

130. What are the core elements of the CCNP business case?
<--- Score

131. What are the rough order estimates on cost savings/opportunities that CCNP brings?
<--- Score

132. Is the scope of CCNP defined?
<--- Score

133. What is the scope of the CCNP effort?

<--- Score

Add up total points for this section:
_____ = Total points for this section

Divided by: _____ (number of
statements answered) = _____
Average score for this section

Transfer your score to the CCNP Index at
the beginning of the Self-Assessment.

CRITERION #3: MEASURE:

INTENT: Gather the correct data.
Measure the current performance and
evolution of the situation.

In my belief, the answer to this
question is clearly defined:

5 Strongly Agree

4 Agree

3 Neutral

2 Disagree

1 Strongly Disagree

1. Are the measurements objective?
<--- Score

2. Has a cost center been established?
<--- Score

3. What users will be impacted?
<--- Score

4. Does management have the right priorities among projects?
<--- Score

5. How long to keep data and how to manage retention costs?
<--- Score

6. What are the CCNP key cost drivers?
<--- Score

7. What evidence is there and what is measured?
<--- Score

8. What is the cost of rework?
<--- Score

9. What is your decision requirements diagram?
<--- Score

10. What methods are feasible and acceptable to estimate the impact of reforms?
<--- Score

11. What is the root cause(s) of the problem?
<--- Score

12. How do you measure lifecycle phases?
<--- Score

13. Do the benefits outweigh the costs?
<--- Score

14. Where is the cost?
<--- Score

15. What would be a real cause for concern?
<--- Score

16. What are hidden CCNP quality costs?
<--- Score

17. What are the costs of reform?
<--- Score

18. Are there competing CCNP priorities?
<--- Score

19. Do you have any cost CCNP limitation requirements?
<--- Score

20. Among the CCNP product and service cost to be estimated, which is considered hardest to estimate?
<--- Score

21. How do you quantify and qualify impacts?
<--- Score

22. How do you verify your resources?
<--- Score

23. How will you measure success?
<--- Score

24. What are allowable costs?
<--- Score

25. What does verifying compliance entail?
<--- Score

26. How will you measure your CCNP effectiveness?

<--- Score

27. Have you made assumptions about the shape of the future, particularly its impact on your customers and competitors?
<--- Score

28. How can you reduce the costs of obtaining inputs?
<--- Score

29. What happens if cost savings do not materialize?
<--- Score

30. How do you verify the CCNP requirements quality?
<--- Score

31. How do you measure success?
<--- Score

32. When a disaster occurs, who gets priority?
<--- Score

33. What are your customers expectations and measures?
<--- Score

34. Why do you expend time and effort to implement measurement, for whom?
<--- Score

35. What causes mismanagement?
<--- Score

36. Is the solution cost-effective?
<--- Score

37. What are the estimated costs of proposed changes?
<--- Score

38. How can a CCNP test verify your ideas or assumptions?
<--- Score

39. Are missed CCNP opportunities costing your organization money?
<--- Score

40. How is the value delivered by CCNP being measured?
<--- Score

41. Where is it measured?
<--- Score

42. What is the total fixed cost?
<--- Score

43. How do your measurements capture actionable CCNP information for use in exceeding your customers expectations and securing your customers engagement?
<--- Score

44. How do you verify the authenticity of the data and information used?
<--- Score

45. How much does it cost?
<--- Score

46. How will success or failure be measured?

<--- Score

47. How can you manage cost down?
<--- Score

48. How do you measure efficient delivery of CCNP services?
<--- Score

49. Are you aware of what could cause a problem?
<--- Score

50. What are you verifying?
<--- Score

51. What are your key CCNP organizational performance measures, including key short and longer-term financial measures?
<--- Score

52. What are the CCNP investment costs?
<--- Score

53. Was a business case (cost/benefit) developed?
<--- Score

54. How frequently do you verify your CCNP strategy?
<--- Score

55. How can you reduce costs?
<--- Score

56. Are there measurements based on task performance?
<--- Score

57. Are the units of measure consistent?
<--- Score

58. Who should receive measurement reports?
<--- Score

59. Why do the measurements/indicators matter?
<--- Score

60. Do you have an issue in getting priority?
<--- Score

61. What are the costs?
<--- Score

62. What are the costs of delaying CCNP action?
<--- Score

63. What does losing customers cost your organization?
<--- Score

64. What are your operating costs?
<--- Score

65. How do you measure variability?
<--- Score

66. Are CCNP vulnerabilities categorized and prioritized?
<--- Score

67. Does a CCNP quantification method exist?
<--- Score

68. What potential environmental factors impact the

CCNP effort?
<--- Score

69. What do you measure and why?
<--- Score

70. What measurements are possible, practicable and meaningful?
<--- Score

71. What are the costs and benefits?
<--- Score

72. What are the operational costs after CCNP deployment?
<--- Score

73. How do you aggregate measures across priorities?
<--- Score

74. What do people want to verify?
<--- Score

75. How do you verify and develop ideas and innovations?
<--- Score

76. How sensitive must the CCNP strategy be to cost?
<--- Score

77. Will CCNP have an impact on current business continuity, disaster recovery processes and/or infrastructure?
<--- Score

78. What does your operating model cost?

<--- Score

79. What are the strategic priorities for this year?
<--- Score

80. Are you taking your company in the direction of better and revenue or cheaper and cost?
<--- Score

81. How do you prevent mis-estimating cost?
<--- Score

82. How do you verify and validate the CCNP data?
<--- Score

83. Have you included everything in your CCNP cost models?
<--- Score

84. What does a Test Case verify?
<--- Score

85. Is the cost worth the CCNP effort ?
<--- Score

86. Which measures and indicators matter?
<--- Score

87. How are measurements made?
<--- Score

88. How do you verify performance?
<--- Score

89. Did you tackle the cause or the symptom?
<--- Score

90. What drives O&M cost?
<--- Score

91. Where can you go to verify the info?
<--- Score

92. What is the cause of any CCNP gaps?
<--- Score

93. How will effects be measured?
<--- Score

94. Have design-to-cost goals been established?
<--- Score

95. How do you verify CCNP completeness and accuracy?
<--- Score

96. What tests verify requirements?
<--- Score

97. Are the CCNP benefits worth its costs?
<--- Score

98. How is performance measured?
<--- Score

99. How will costs be allocated?
<--- Score

100. What relevant entities could be measured?
<--- Score

101. What causes investor action?

<--- Score

102. How is progress measured?
<--- Score

103. Which CCNP impacts are significant?
<--- Score

104. Is there an opportunity to verify requirements?
<--- Score

105. How do you verify if CCNP is built right?
<--- Score

106. Are you able to realize any cost savings?
<--- Score

107. At what cost?
<--- Score

108. Who pays the cost?
<--- Score

109. What disadvantage does this cause for the user?
<--- Score

110. Are actual costs in line with budgeted costs?
<--- Score

111. When are costs are incurred?
<--- Score

112. What could cause you to change course?
<--- Score

113. What causes innovation to fail or succeed in your

organization?
<--- Score

114. Are indirect costs charged to the CCNP program?
<--- Score

115. Does the CCNP task fit the client's priorities?
<--- Score

116. Do you aggressively reward and promote the people who have the biggest impact on creating excellent CCNP services/products?
<--- Score

117. Who is involved in verifying compliance?
<--- Score

118. How can you measure CCNP in a systematic way?
<--- Score

119. How do you control the overall costs of your work processes?
<--- Score

120. How will measures be used to manage and adapt?
<--- Score

121. What details are required of the CCNP cost structure?
<--- Score

122. Are there any easy-to-implement alternatives to CCNP? Sometimes other solutions are available that do not require the cost implications of a full-blown project?

<--- Score

123. What is measured? Why?
<--- Score

124. What is your CCNP quality cost segregation study?
<--- Score

125. Which is something that can cause issues in a PKI system?
<--- Score

126. What harm might be caused?
<--- Score

127. What is the CCNP business impact?
<--- Score

128. How will your organization measure success?
<--- Score

129. What are the uncertainties surrounding estimates of impact?
<--- Score

130. When should you bother with diagrams?
<--- Score

Add up total points for this section:
_ _ _ _ _ = Total points for this section

Divided by: _ _ _ _ _ _ (number of statements answered) = _ _ _ _ _ _
Average score for this section

Transfer your score to the CCNP Index at
the beginning of the Self-Assessment.

CRITERION #4: ANALYZE:

INTENT: Analyze causes, assumptions and hypotheses.

In my belief, the answer to this question is clearly defined:

5 Strongly Agree

4 Agree

3 Neutral

2 Disagree

1 Strongly Disagree

1. What does the data say about the performance of the stakeholder process?
<--- Score

2. What will drive CCNP change?
<--- Score

3. How do you define collaboration and team output?
<--- Score

4. How can risk management be tied procedurally to process elements?
<--- Score

5. How was the detailed process map generated, verified, and validated?
<--- Score

6. What were the crucial 'moments of truth' on the process map?
<--- Score

7. What are the processes for audit reporting and management?
<--- Score

8. Do your employees have the opportunity to do what they do best everyday?
<--- Score

9. What are the personnel training and qualifications required?
<--- Score

10. How is data used for program management and improvement?
<--- Score

11. How difficult is it to qualify what CCNP ROI is?
<--- Score

12. What is your organizations process which leads to recognition of value generation?
<--- Score

13. What kind of crime could a potential new hire

have committed that would not only not disqualify him/her from being hired by your organization, but would actually indicate that he/she might be a particularly good fit?
<--- Score

14. What systems/processes must you excel at?
<--- Score

15. Is the performance gap determined?
<--- Score

16. Which of the options ensures data integrity in the tunnel?
<--- Score

17. What are your key performance measures or indicators and in-process measures for the control and improvement of your CCNP processes?
<--- Score

18. What is the cost of poor quality as supported by the team's analysis?
<--- Score

19. How will corresponding data be collected?
<--- Score

20. Is data and process analysis, root cause analysis and quantifying the gap/opportunity in place?
<--- Score

21. What qualifies as competition?
<--- Score

22. Record-keeping requirements flow from the

records needed as inputs, outputs, controls and for transformation of a CCNP process, are the records needed as inputs to the CCNP process available?
<--- Score

23. Is there a strict change management process?
<--- Score

24. What process should you select for improvement?
<--- Score

25. What training and qualifications will you need?
<--- Score

26. How do your work systems and key work processes relate to and capitalize on your core competencies?
<--- Score

27. Who will facilitate the team and process?
<--- Score

28. When should a process be art not science?
<--- Score

29. What is the output?
<--- Score

30. What are the CCNP design outputs?
<--- Score

31. Have any additional benefits been identified that will result from closing all or most of the gaps?
<--- Score

32. How do you implement and manage your

work processes to ensure that they meet design requirements?
<--- Score

33. Is the required CCNP data gathered?
<--- Score

34. How do mission and objectives affect the CCNP processes of your organization?
<--- Score

35. What are the revised rough estimates of the financial savings/opportunity for CCNP improvements?
<--- Score

36. What are the necessary qualifications?
<--- Score

37. Who gets your output?
<--- Score

38. What information qualified as important?
<--- Score

39. Is the final output clearly identified?
<--- Score

40. What conclusions were drawn from the team's data collection and analysis? How did the team reach these conclusions?
<--- Score

41. How is the data gathered?
<--- Score

42. What tools were used to narrow the list of possible causes?
<--- Score

43. What are your current levels and trends in key measures or indicators of CCNP product and process performance that are important to and directly serve your customers? How do these results compare with the performance of your competitors and other organizations with similar offerings?
<--- Score

44. Has data output been validated?
<--- Score

45. Do staff qualifications match your project?
<--- Score

46. What controls do you have in place to protect data?
<--- Score

47. What internal processes need improvement?
<--- Score

48. Have the problem and goal statements been updated to reflect the additional knowledge gained from the analyze phase?
<--- Score

49. Is there an established change management process?
<--- Score

50. Do several people in different organizational units assist with the CCNP process?

<--- Score

51. What other jobs or tasks affect the performance of the steps in the CCNP process?
<--- Score

52. What is your organizations system for selecting qualified vendors?
<--- Score

53. Is the CCNP process severely broken such that a re-design is necessary?
<--- Score

54. Were Pareto charts (or similar) used to portray the 'heavy hitters' (or key sources of variation)?
<--- Score

55. How do you ensure that the CCNP opportunity is realistic?
<--- Score

56. How is the way you as the leader think and process information affecting your organizational culture?
<--- Score

57. What CCNP data will be collected?
<--- Score

58. What, related to, CCNP processes does your organization outsource?
<--- Score

59. Was a detailed process map created to amplify critical steps of the 'as is' stakeholder process?
<--- Score

60. Is the suppliers process defined and controlled?
<--- Score

61. Which command is used at an end system to correct problems at the data link layer relating to resolving network and data link layer addresses?
<--- Score

62. How often will data be collected for measures?
<--- Score

63. What CCNP metrics are outputs of the process?
<--- Score

64. Can you add value to the current CCNP decision-making process (largely qualitative) by incorporating uncertainty modeling (more quantitative)?
<--- Score

65. How do you promote understanding that opportunity for improvement is not criticism of the status quo, or the people who created the status quo?
<--- Score

66. Are gaps between current performance and the goal performance identified?
<--- Score

67. What output to create?
<--- Score

68. Who owns what data?
<--- Score

69. Identify an operational issue in your organization,

for example, could a particular task be done more quickly or more efficiently by CCNP?
<--- Score

70. Was a cause-and-effect diagram used to explore the different types of causes (or sources of variation)?
<--- Score

71. What CCNP data should be managed?
<--- Score

72. Have you defined which data is gathered how?
<--- Score

73. Should you invest in industry-recognized qualifications?
<--- Score

74. What are your outputs?
<--- Score

75. What are your CCNP processes?
<--- Score

76. How will the CCNP data be captured?
<--- Score

77. Are your outputs consistent?
<--- Score

78. Did any value-added analysis or 'lean thinking' take place to identify some of the gaps shown on the 'as is' process map?
<--- Score

79. Do you, as a leader, bounce back quickly from

setbacks?
<--- Score

80. How are outputs preserved and protected?
<--- Score

81. How do you use CCNP data and information to support organizational decision making and innovation?
<--- Score

82. What other organizational variables, such as reward systems or communication systems, affect the performance of this CCNP process?
<--- Score

83. What qualifications are necessary?
<--- Score

84. Where is the data coming from to measure compliance?
<--- Score

85. Who qualifies to gain access to data?
<--- Score

86. How do you identify specific CCNP investment opportunities and emerging trends?
<--- Score

87. What are the disruptive CCNP technologies that enable your organization to radically change your business processes?
<--- Score

88. What did the team gain from developing a sub-

process map?
<--- Score

89. What are your current levels and trends in key CCNP measures or indicators of product and process performance that are important to and directly serve your customers?
<--- Score

90. What methods do you use to gather CCNP data?
<--- Score

91. What do you need to qualify?
<--- Score

92. Do your leaders quickly bounce back from setbacks?
<--- Score

93. What quality tools were used to get through the analyze phase?
<--- Score

94. A compounding model resolution with available relevant data can often provide insight towards a solution methodology; which CCNP models, tools and techniques are necessary?
<--- Score

95. What CCNP data do you gather or use now?
<--- Score

96. How has the CCNP data been gathered?
<--- Score

97. Do you understand your management processes

today?
<--- Score

98. Think about the functions involved in your CCNP project, what processes flow from these functions?
<--- Score

99. Who will gather what data?
<--- Score

100. Are you missing CCNP opportunities?
<--- Score

101. What is the CCNP Driver?
<--- Score

102. What is the Value Stream Mapping?
<--- Score

103. Who is involved in the management review process?
<--- Score

104. Were there any improvement opportunities identified from the process analysis?
<--- Score

105. Are CCNP changes recognized early enough to be approved through the regular process?
<--- Score

106. How much data can be collected in the given timeframe?
<--- Score

107. What successful thing are you doing today that

may be blinding you to new growth opportunities?
<--- Score

108. What are evaluation criteria for the output?
<--- Score

109. What are the best opportunities for value improvement?
<--- Score

110. What are your best practices for minimizing CCNP project risk, while demonstrating incremental value and quick wins throughout the CCNP project lifecycle?
<--- Score

111. What resources go in to get the desired output?
<--- Score

112. Are all team members qualified for all tasks?
<--- Score

113. Is the gap/opportunity displayed and communicated in financial terms?
<--- Score

114. How is CCNP data gathered?
<--- Score

115. Were any designed experiments used to generate additional insight into the data analysis?
<--- Score

116. Is pre-qualification of suppliers carried out?
<--- Score

117. Did any additional data need to be collected?
<--- Score

118. Do quality systems drive continuous improvement?
<--- Score

119. Which CCNP data should be retained?
<--- Score

120. An organizationally feasible system request is one that considers the mission, goals and objectives of the organization, key questions are: is the CCNP solution request practical and will it solve a problem or take advantage of an opportunity to achieve company goals?
<--- Score

121. What tools were used to generate the list of possible causes?
<--- Score

122. Has an output goal been set?
<--- Score

123. What were the financial benefits resulting from any 'ground fruit or low-hanging fruit' (quick fixes)?
<--- Score

124. Is there any way to speed up the process?
<--- Score

125. What qualifications are needed?
<--- Score

126. Do you have the authority to produce the

output?

<--- Score

127. Where is CCNP data gathered?
<--- Score

128. How will the data be checked for quality?
<--- Score

129. How is the CCNP Value Stream Mapping managed?
<--- Score

130. What types of data do your CCNP indicators require?
<--- Score

Add up total points for this section:
_____ = Total points for this section

Divided by: _____ (number of statements answered) = _____
Average score for this section

Transfer your score to the CCNP Index at the beginning of the Self-Assessment.

CRITERION #5: IMPROVE:

INTENT: Develop a practical solution. Innovate, establish and test the solution and to measure the results.

In my belief, the answer to this question is clearly defined:

5 Strongly Agree

4 Agree

3 Neutral

2 Disagree

1 Strongly Disagree

1. How do the CCNP results compare with the performance of your competitors and other organizations with similar offerings?
<--- Score

2. How do you measure risk?
<--- Score

3. What practices helps your organization to develop

its capacity to recognize patterns?
<--- Score

4. How can skill-level changes improve CCNP?
<--- Score

5. What tools were used to tap into the creativity and encourage 'outside the box' thinking?
<--- Score

6. Are procedures documented for managing CCNP risks?
<--- Score

7. Do you cover the five essential competencies: Communication, Collaboration,Innovation, Adaptability, and Leadership that improve an organizations ability to leverage the new CCNP in a volatile global economy?
<--- Score

8. How is knowledge sharing about risk management improved?
<--- Score

9. What CCNP improvements can be made?
<--- Score

10. How does your organization evaluate strategic CCNP success?
<--- Score

11. How do you measure improved CCNP service perception, and satisfaction?
<--- Score

12. Is the CCNP documentation thorough?
<--- Score

13. Can you identify any significant risks or exposures to CCNP third- parties (vendors, service providers, alliance partners etc) that concern you?
<--- Score

14. How will you know when its improved?
<--- Score

15. How do you link measurement and risk?
<--- Score

16. What area needs the greatest improvement?
<--- Score

17. Would you develop a CCNP Communication Strategy?
<--- Score

18. What are the concrete CCNP results?
<--- Score

19. Who manages supplier risk management in your organization?
<--- Score

20. What current systems have to be understood and/ or changed?
<--- Score

21. To what extent does management recognize CCNP as a tool to increase the results?
<--- Score

22. Do those selected for the CCNP team have a good general understanding of what CCNP is all about?
<--- Score

23. Do you need to do a usability evaluation?
<--- Score

24. Risk events: what are the things that could go wrong?
<--- Score

25. Was a pilot designed for the proposed solution(s)?
<--- Score

26. How do you improve your likelihood of success ?
<--- Score

27. Is there a small-scale pilot for proposed improvement(s)? What conclusions were drawn from the outcomes of a pilot?
<--- Score

28. Can the solution be designed and implemented within an acceptable time period?
<--- Score

29. What is the implementation plan?
<--- Score

30. For decision problems, how do you develop a decision statement?
<--- Score

31. Does a good decision guarantee a good outcome?
<--- Score

32. How can you better manage risk?
<--- Score

33. What are your current levels and trends in key measures or indicators of workforce and leader development?
<--- Score

34. What alternative responses are available to manage risk?
<--- Score

35. What is the magnitude of the improvements?
<--- Score

36. What resources are required for the improvement efforts?
<--- Score

37. How are CCNP risks managed?
<--- Score

38. What attendant changes will need to be made to ensure that the solution is successful?
<--- Score

39. Who controls key decisions that will be made?
<--- Score

40. What tools were most useful during the improve phase?
<--- Score

41. Why improve in the first place?
<--- Score

42. What is the team's contingency plan for potential problems occurring in implementation?
<--- Score

43. Are risk management tasks balanced centrally and locally?
<--- Score

44. If you could go back in time five years, what decision would you make differently? What is your best guess as to what decision you're making today you might regret five years from now?
<--- Score

45. Is the optimal solution selected based on testing and analysis?
<--- Score

46. Are the risks fully understood, reasonable and manageable?
<--- Score

47. Is the CCNP risk managed?
<--- Score

48. How do you mitigate CCNP risk?
<--- Score

49. Who are the CCNP decision-makers?
<--- Score

50. What can you do to improve?
<--- Score

51. How do you define the solutions' scope?
<--- Score

52. Is risk periodically assessed?
<--- Score

53. Explorations of the frontiers of CCNP will help you build influence, improve CCNP, optimize decision making, and sustain change, what is your approach?
<--- Score

54. Is any CCNP documentation required?
<--- Score

55. How are policy decisions made and where?
<--- Score

56. How is continuous improvement applied to risk management?
<--- Score

57. Who should make the CCNP decisions?
<--- Score

58. Are the key business and technology risks being managed?
<--- Score

59. Who are the key stakeholders for the CCNP evaluation?
<--- Score

60. What were the underlying assumptions on the cost-benefit analysis?
<--- Score

61. Are events managed to resolution?
<--- Score

62. What is the CCNP's sustainability risk?
<--- Score

63. For estimation problems, how do you develop an estimation statement?
<--- Score

64. Risk Identification: What are the possible risk events your organization faces in relation to CCNP?
<--- Score

65. What is CCNP's impact on utilizing the best solution(s)?
<--- Score

66. What error proofing will be done to address some of the discrepancies observed in the 'as is' process?
<--- Score

67. What is the risk?
<--- Score

68. What assumptions are made about the solution and approach?
<--- Score

69. Who controls the risk?
<--- Score

70. CCNP risk decisions: whose call Is It?
<--- Score

71. How do you manage and improve your CCNP work systems to deliver customer value and achieve organizational success and sustainability?

<--- Score

72. What is CCNP risk?
<--- Score

73. Which of the recognised risks out of all risks can be most likely transferred?
<--- Score

74. How do you keep improving CCNP?
<--- Score

75. Who will be responsible for documenting the CCNP requirements in detail?
<--- Score

76. What strategies for CCNP improvement are successful?
<--- Score

77. Who will be responsible for making the decisions to include or exclude requested changes once CCNP is underway?
<--- Score

78. Do you combine technical expertise with business knowledge and CCNP Key topics include lifecycles, development approaches, requirements and how to make a business case?
<--- Score

79. What to do with the results or outcomes of measurements?
<--- Score

80. What criteria will you use to assess your CCNP

risks?
<--- Score

81. Is the CCNP solution sustainable?
<--- Score

82. Who do you report CCNP results to?
<--- Score

83. What do you want to improve?
<--- Score

84. What are the affordable CCNP risks?
<--- Score

85. Will the controls trigger any other risks?
<--- Score

86. How can you improve performance?
<--- Score

87. How do you go about comparing CCNP approaches/solutions?
<--- Score

88. What does the 'should be' process map/design look like?
<--- Score

89. What were the criteria for evaluating a CCNP pilot?
<--- Score

90. Do you have the optimal project management team structure?
<--- Score

91. How significant is the improvement in the eyes of the end user?
<--- Score

92. Have you achieved CCNP improvements?
<--- Score

93. Is there a high likelihood that any recommendations will achieve their intended results?
<--- Score

94. Are decisions made in a timely manner?
<--- Score

95. What are the expected CCNP results?
<--- Score

96. Who manages CCNP risk?
<--- Score

97. Is the scope clearly documented?
<--- Score

98. Was a CCNP charter developed?
<--- Score

99. How scalable is your CCNP solution?
<--- Score

100. Is the solution technically practical?
<--- Score

101. How can you improve CCNP?
<--- Score

102. How will you measure the results?

<--- Score

103. How does the team improve its work?
<--- Score

104. Who will be using the results of the measurement activities?
<--- Score

105. Do vendor agreements bring new compliance risk ?
<--- Score

106. How risky is your organization?
<--- Score

107. Can you integrate quality management and risk management?
<--- Score

108. When you map the key players in your own work and the types/domains of relationships with them, which relationships do you find easy and which challenging, and why?
<--- Score

109. Is there any other CCNP solution?
<--- Score

110. Where do you need CCNP improvement?
<--- Score

111. Are the most efficient solutions problem-specific?
<--- Score

112. What communications are necessary to support

the implementation of the solution?
<--- Score

113. At what point will vulnerability assessments be performed once CCNP is put into production (e.g., ongoing Risk Management after implementation)?
<--- Score

114. Who are the CCNP decision makers?
<--- Score

115. How can the phases of CCNP development be identified?
<--- Score

116. Have you identified breakpoints and/or risk tolerances that will trigger broad consideration of a potential need for intervention or modification of strategy?
<--- Score

117. Where do the CCNP decisions reside?
<--- Score

118. What needs improvement? Why?
<--- Score

119. What tools were used to evaluate the potential solutions?
<--- Score

120. Does the goal represent a desired result that can be measured?
<--- Score

121. Is there a cost/benefit analysis of optimal

solution(s)?
<--- Score

122. What are the CCNP security risks?
<--- Score

123. Who makes the CCNP decisions in your organization?
<--- Score

124. What should a proof of concept or pilot accomplish?
<--- Score

125. Is CCNP documentation maintained?
<--- Score

126. Were any criteria developed to assist the team in testing and evaluating potential solutions?
<--- Score

127. Is the measure of success for CCNP understandable to a variety of people?
<--- Score

128. Risk factors: what are the characteristics of CCNP that make it risky?
<--- Score

129. How do you improve productivity?
<--- Score

130. Are risk triggers captured?
<--- Score

131. How do you decide how much to remunerate an

employee?

<--- Score

132. How do you manage CCNP risk?

<--- Score

133. What risks do you need to manage?

<--- Score

134. What lessons, if any, from a pilot were incorporated into the design of the full-scale solution?

<--- Score

135. What tools do you use once you have decided on a CCNP strategy and more importantly how do you choose?

<--- Score

136. How do you deal with CCNP risk?

<--- Score

137. Are you assessing CCNP and risk?

<--- Score

138. How will you know that you have improved?

<--- Score

Add up total points for this section:

_ _ _ _ _ = Total points for this section

Divided by: _ _ _ _ _ _ (number of statements answered) = _ _ _ _ _ _ Average score for this section

Transfer your score to the CCNP Index at the beginning of the Self-Assessment.

CRITERION #6: CONTROL:

INTENT: Implement the practical solution. Maintain the performance and correct possible complications.

In my belief, the answer to this question is clearly defined:

5 Strongly Agree

4 Agree

3 Neutral

2 Disagree

1 Strongly Disagree

1. What is the recommended frequency of auditing?
<--- Score

2. How do your controls stack up?
<--- Score

3. What do you stand for--and what are you against?
<--- Score

4. How do you plan on providing proper recognition and disclosure of supporting companies?
<--- Score

5. Does a troubleshooting guide exist or is it needed?
<--- Score

6. Is knowledge gained on process shared and institutionalized?
<--- Score

7. Will any special training be provided for results interpretation?
<--- Score

8. What is the best design framework for CCNP organization now that, in a post industrial-age if the top-down, command and control model is no longer relevant?
<--- Score

9. Is new knowledge gained imbedded in the response plan?
<--- Score

10. Have new or revised work instructions resulted?
<--- Score

11. Has the improved process and its steps been standardized?
<--- Score

12. How is CCNP project cost planned, managed, monitored?
<--- Score

13. What other systems, operations, processes, and infrastructures (hiring practices, staffing, training, incentives/rewards, metrics/dashboards/scorecards, etc.) need updates, additions, changes, or deletions in order to facilitate knowledge transfer and improvements?
<--- Score

14. How can you best use all of your knowledge repositories to enhance learning and sharing?
<--- Score

15. Do you monitor the CCNP decisions made and fine tune them as they evolve?
<--- Score

16. Does CCNP appropriately measure and monitor risk?
<--- Score

17. What is the control/monitoring plan?
<--- Score

18. Who will be in control?
<--- Score

19. Is there documentation that will support the successful operation of the improvement?
<--- Score

20. Is the CCNP test/monitoring cost justified?
<--- Score

21. How will report readings be checked to effectively monitor performance?
<--- Score

22. Is there a recommended audit plan for routine surveillance inspections of CCNP's gains?
<--- Score

23. Are documented procedures clear and easy to follow for the operators?
<--- Score

24. Are controls in place and consistently applied?
<--- Score

25. How will input, process, and output variables be checked to detect for sub-optimal conditions?
<--- Score

26. How will CCNP decisions be made and monitored?
<--- Score

27. Are pertinent alerts monitored, analyzed and distributed to appropriate personnel?
<--- Score

28. Who is the CCNP process owner?
<--- Score

29. Does the response plan contain a definite closed loop continual improvement scheme (e.g., plan-do-check-act)?
<--- Score

30. What other areas of the group might benefit from the CCNP team's improvements, knowledge, and learning?
<--- Score

31. How do you monitor usage and cost?
<--- Score

32. What are the known security controls?
<--- Score

33. Is there a control plan in place for sustaining improvements (short and long-term)?
<--- Score

34. How do you spread information?
<--- Score

35. What quality tools were useful in the control phase?
<--- Score

36. What should the next improvement project be that is related to CCNP?
<--- Score

37. What adjustments to the strategies are needed?
<--- Score

38. What is your theory of human motivation, and how does your compensation plan fit with that view?
<--- Score

39. Who is going to spread your message?
<--- Score

40. Are there documented procedures?
<--- Score

41. How will the day-to-day responsibilities for monitoring and continual improvement be

transferred from the improvement team to the process owner?
<--- Score

42. Is there a standardized process?
<--- Score

43. Where do ideas that reach policy makers and planners as proposals for CCNP strengthening and reform actually originate?
<--- Score

44. Against what alternative is success being measured?
<--- Score

45. What key inputs and outputs are being measured on an ongoing basis?
<--- Score

46. How might the group capture best practices and lessons learned so as to leverage improvements?
<--- Score

47. What should you measure to verify efficiency gains?
<--- Score

48. What can you control?
<--- Score

49. Are operating procedures consistent?
<--- Score

50. How is change control managed?
<--- Score

51. How likely is the current CCNP plan to come in on schedule or on budget?
<--- Score

52. Who sets the CCNP standards?
<--- Score

53. Is there a transfer of ownership and knowledge to process owner and process team tasked with the responsibilities.
<--- Score

54. Act/Adjust: What Do you Need to Do Differently?
<--- Score

55. How do you establish and deploy modified action plans if circumstances require a shift in plans and rapid execution of new plans?
<--- Score

56. Implementation Planning: is a pilot needed to test the changes before a full roll out occurs?
<--- Score

57. How will new or emerging customer needs/requirements be checked/communicated to orient the process toward meeting the new specifications and continually reducing variation?
<--- Score

58. Is there a documented and implemented monitoring plan?
<--- Score

59. Is there an action plan in case of emergencies?

<--- Score

60. Who has control over resources?
<--- Score

61. How will you measure your QA plan's
effectiveness?
<--- Score

62. Is there a CCNP Communication plan covering
who needs to get what information when?
<--- Score

63. How do controls support value?
<--- Score

64. Will existing staff require re-training, for example,
to learn new business processes?
<--- Score

65. Is a response plan established and deployed?
<--- Score

66. How will the process owner verify improvement in
present and future sigma levels, process capabilities?
<--- Score

67. Are you measuring, monitoring and predicting
CCNP activities to optimize operations and
profitability, and enhancing outcomes?
<--- Score

68. You may have created your quality measures at a
time when you lacked resources, technology wasn't
up to the required standard, or low service levels
were the industry norm. Have those circumstances

changed?
<--- Score

69. Can you adapt and adjust to changing CCNP situations?
<--- Score

70. How widespread is its use?
<--- Score

71. Are the CCNP standards challenging?
<--- Score

72. In the case of a CCNP project, the criteria for the audit derive from implementation objectives, an audit of a CCNP project involves assessing whether the recommendations outlined for implementation have been met, can you track that any CCNP project is implemented as planned, and is it working?
<--- Score

73. What are you attempting to measure/monitor?
<--- Score

74. What do you measure to verify effectiveness gains?
<--- Score

75. Do the CCNP decisions you make today help people and the planet tomorrow?
<--- Score

76. How will the process owner and team be able to hold the gains?
<--- Score

77. What are the performance and scale of the CCNP tools?
<--- Score

78. Are suggested corrective/restorative actions indicated on the response plan for known causes to problems that might surface?
<--- Score

79. Do the viable solutions scale to future needs?
<--- Score

80. Are the planned controls in place?
<--- Score

81. Is a response plan in place for when the input, process, or output measures indicate an 'out-of-control' condition?
<--- Score

82. What are customers monitoring?
<--- Score

83. How do you plan for the cost of succession?
<--- Score

84. Who controls critical resources?
<--- Score

85. Will the team be available to assist members in planning investigations?
<--- Score

86. Is reporting being used or needed?
<--- Score

87. Has the CCNP value of standards been quantified?
<--- Score

88. Are the planned controls working?
<--- Score

89. What CCNP standards are applicable?
<--- Score

90. What is your plan to assess your security risks?
<--- Score

91. Does the CCNP performance meet the customer's requirements?
<--- Score

92. What are the critical parameters to watch?
<--- Score

93. What are your results for key measures or indicators of the accomplishment of your CCNP strategy and action plans, including building and strengthening core competencies?
<--- Score

94. How do you select, collect, align, and integrate CCNP data and information for tracking daily operations and overall organizational performance, including progress relative to strategic objectives and action plans?
<--- Score

95. Can support from partners be adjusted?
<--- Score

96. Are new process steps, standards, and

documentation ingrained into normal operations?
<--- Score

97. What are the key elements of your CCNP performance improvement system, including your evaluation, organizational learning, and innovation processes?
<--- Score

98. How do you encourage people to take control and responsibility?
<--- Score

99. Does job training on the documented procedures need to be part of the process team's education and training?
<--- Score

Add up total points for this section:
_____ = Total points for this section

Divided by: _____ (number of statements answered) = _____
Average score for this section

Transfer your score to the CCNP Index at the beginning of the Self-Assessment.

CRITERION #7: SUSTAIN:

INTENT: Retain the benefits.

In my belief, the answer to this question is clearly defined:

5 Strongly Agree

4 Agree

3 Neutral

2 Disagree

1 Strongly Disagree

1. What was the last experiment you ran?
<--- Score

2. What is something you believe that nearly no one agrees with you on?
<--- Score

3. What knowledge, skills and characteristics mark a good CCNP project manager?
<--- Score

4. Who do you think the world wants your organization to be?
<--- Score

5. Do you have enough freaky customers in your portfolio pushing you to the limit day in and day out?
<--- Score

6. Are you paying enough attention to the partners your company depends on to succeed?
<--- Score

7. How do you govern and fulfill your societal responsibilities?
<--- Score

8. Why should people listen to you?
<--- Score

9. What happens at your organization when people fail?
<--- Score

10. How do you ensure that implementations of CCNP products are done in a way that ensures safety?
<--- Score

11. Is there a work around that you can use?
<--- Score

12. Can you break it down?
<--- Score

13. What is the overall business strategy?
<--- Score

14. What role does communication play in the success or failure of a CCNP project?
<--- Score

15. If your customer were your grandmother, would you tell her to buy what you're selling?
<--- Score

16. What new services of functionality will be implemented next with CCNP ?
<--- Score

17. Were lessons learned captured and communicated?
<--- Score

18. Why do and why don't your customers like your organization?
<--- Score

19. What are current CCNP paradigms?
<--- Score

20. Do you have past CCNP successes?
<--- Score

21. What happens when a new employee joins the organization?
<--- Score

22. How do you transition from the baseline to the target?
<--- Score

23. Ask yourself: how would you do this work if you only had one staff member to do it?

<--- Score

24. Are new benefits received and understood?
<--- Score

25. Who do we want your customers to become?
<--- Score

26. What threat is CCNP addressing?
<--- Score

27. How will you motivate the stakeholders with the least vested interest?
<--- Score

28. In the past year, what have you done (or could you have done) to increase the accurate perception of your company/brand as ethical and honest?
<--- Score

29. How do switches segment a network?
<--- Score

30. To whom do you add value?
<--- Score

31. Who are the key stakeholders?
<--- Score

32. Can you maintain your growth without detracting from the factors that have contributed to your success?
<--- Score

33. Are assumptions made in CCNP stated explicitly?
<--- Score

34. What are strategies for increasing support and reducing opposition?

<--- Score

35. How do you configure a static IPv6 default route?

<--- Score

36. What are the business goals CCNP is aiming to achieve?

<--- Score

37. What are efficient methods of troubleshooting a network failure?

<--- Score

38. Who are four people whose careers you have enhanced?

<--- Score

39. Political -is anyone trying to undermine this project?

<--- Score

40. How will you ensure you get what you expected?

<--- Score

41. Who else should you help?

<--- Score

42. How much does CCNP help?

<--- Score

43. What is the craziest thing you can do?

<--- Score

44. If there were zero limitations, what would you do differently?

<--- Score

45. What is your formula for success in CCNP ?

<--- Score

46. Who is on the team?

<--- Score

47. What could happen if you do not do it?

<--- Score

48. Have benefits been optimized with all key stakeholders?

<--- Score

49. Are you making progress, and are you making progress as CCNP leaders?

<--- Score

50. Who, on the executive team or the board, has spoken to a customer recently?

<--- Score

51. Do you think CCNP accomplishes the goals you expect it to accomplish?

<--- Score

52. Where can you break convention?

<--- Score

53. Are you using a design thinking approach and integrating Innovation, CCNP Experience, and Brand Value?

<--- Score

54. What projects are going on in the organization today, and what resources are those projects using from the resource pools?
<--- Score

55. What is your question? Why?
<--- Score

56. What is phishing and why is it a threat?
<--- Score

57. What are the key enablers to make this CCNP move?
<--- Score

58. How do you cross-sell and up-sell your CCNP success?
<--- Score

59. When information truly is ubiquitous, when reach and connectivity are completely global, when computing resources are infinite, and when a whole new set of impossibilities are not only possible, but happening, what will that do to your business?
<--- Score

60. How do you know if you are successful?
<--- Score

61. What do we do when new problems arise?
<--- Score

62. What are the challenges?
<--- Score

63. How do you foster innovation?
<--- Score

64. How do you manage CCNP Knowledge Management (KM)?
<--- Score

65. Is CCNP realistic, or are you setting yourself up for failure?
<--- Score

66. Are the criteria for selecting recommendations stated?
<--- Score

67. How do you stay inspired?
<--- Score

68. Whose voice (department, ethnic group, women, older workers, etc) might you have missed hearing from in your company, and how might you amplify this voice to create positive momentum for your business?
<--- Score

69. What is the estimated value of the project?
<--- Score

70. If no one would ever find out about your accomplishments, how would you lead differently?
<--- Score

71. How do you deal with CCNP changes?
<--- Score

72. How do you proactively clarify deliverables and CCNP quality expectations?
<--- Score

73. Do you know what you are doing? And who do you call if you don't?
<--- Score

74. What have been your experiences in defining long range CCNP goals?
<--- Score

75. If you had to rebuild your organization without any traditional competitive advantages (i.e., no killer technology, promising research, innovative product/ service delivery model, etcetera), how would your people have to approach their work and collaborate together in order to create the necessary conditions for success?
<--- Score

76. How can you become the company that would put you out of business?
<--- Score

77. How are you doing compared to your industry?
<--- Score

78. What are the potential basics of CCNP fraud?
<--- Score

79. Which individuals, teams or departments will be involved in CCNP?
<--- Score

80. How do you provide a safe environment

-physically and emotionally?
<--- Score

81. Which cisco switch products should be used in the distribution layer of a campus network?
<--- Score

82. If you find that you havent accomplished one of the goals for one of the steps of the CCNP strategy, what will you do to fix it?
<--- Score

83. How do you determine the key elements that affect CCNP workforce satisfaction, how are these elements determined for different workforce groups and segments?
<--- Score

84. What is the recommended frequency of auditing?
<--- Score

85. How long will it take to change?
<--- Score

86. What trouble can you get into?
<--- Score

87. What does your signature ensure?
<--- Score

88. If you weren't already in this business, would you enter it today? And if not, what are you going to do about it?
<--- Score

89. Are your responses positive or negative?

<--- Score

90. What are the barriers to increased CCNP production?
<--- Score

91. Have new benefits been realized?
<--- Score

92. Marketing budgets are tighter, consumers are more skeptical, and social media has changed forever the way we talk about CCNP, how do you gain traction?
<--- Score

93. How can you become more high-tech but still be high touch?
<--- Score

94. What is your competitive advantage?
<--- Score

95. How much contingency will be available in the budget?
<--- Score

96. What are the rules and assumptions your industry operates under? What if the opposite were true?
<--- Score

97. Are you satisfied with your current role? If not, what is missing from it?
<--- Score

98. Which CCNP goals are the most important?
<--- Score

99. Will it be accepted by users?
<--- Score

100. Are the assumptions believable and achievable?
<--- Score

101. How do you maintain CCNP's Integrity?
<--- Score

102. What do your reports reflect?
<--- Score

103. How do you create buy-in?
<--- Score

104. What information is critical to your organization that your executives are ignoring?
<--- Score

105. Do you have an implicit bias for capital investments over people investments?
<--- Score

106. Which type of firewall best provides a rich set of application layer inspection capabilities?
<--- Score

107. Which SNMP components is run directly on the device?
<--- Score

108. What you are going to do to affect the numbers?
<--- Score

109. What is the funding source for this project?

<--- Score

110. How will you know that the CCNP project has been successful?
<--- Score

111. What is it like to work for you?
<--- Score

112. What is the ideal relationship between network maintenance and troubleshooting?
<--- Score

113. What must you excel at?
<--- Score

114. What are specific CCNP rules to follow?
<--- Score

115. Can the schedule be done in the given time?
<--- Score

116. If you do not follow, then how to lead?
<--- Score

117. What are the advantages in achieving CCNP Security?
<--- Score

118. Is the CCNP organization completing tasks effectively and efficiently?
<--- Score

119. What trophy do you want on your mantle?
<--- Score

120. Can you do all this work?
<--- Score

121. Why is it important to have senior management support for a CCNP project?
<--- Score

122. If your company went out of business tomorrow, would anyone who doesn't get a paycheck here care?
<--- Score

123. Who is responsible for errors?
<--- Score

124. Who have you, as a company, historically been when you've been at your best?
<--- Score

125. Are you maintaining a past–present–future perspective throughout the CCNP discussion?
<--- Score

126. What are the long-term CCNP goals?
<--- Score

127. How do you lead with CCNP in mind?
<--- Score

128. Who will provide the final approval of CCNP deliverables?
<--- Score

129. How can you negotiate CCNP successfully with a stubborn boss, an irate client, or a deceitful coworker?
<--- Score

130. Do you see more potential in people than they do in themselves?
<--- Score

131. How will you insure seamless interoperability of CCNP moving forward?
<--- Score

132. What CCNP modifications can you make work for you?
<--- Score

133. What are the essentials of internal CCNP management?
<--- Score

134. How do you track customer value, profitability or financial return, organizational success, and sustainability?
<--- Score

135. Why is CCNP important for you now?
<--- Score

136. Who is responsible for ensuring appropriate resources (time, people and money) are allocated to CCNP?
<--- Score

137. How do customers see your organization?
<--- Score

138. Are you / should you be revolutionary or evolutionary?
<--- Score

139. How do you keep records, of what?
<--- Score

140. Instead of going to current contacts for new ideas, what if you reconnected with dormant contacts--the people you used to know? If you were going reactivate a dormant tie, who would it be?
<--- Score

141. What are your personal philosophies regarding CCNP and how do they influence your work?
<--- Score

142. What is a feasible sequencing of reform initiatives over time?
<--- Score

143. In a project to restructure CCNP outcomes, which stakeholders would you involve?
<--- Score

144. Do you have the right capabilities and capacities?
<--- Score

145. Operational - will it work?
<--- Score

146. Is the impact that CCNP has shown?
<--- Score

147. Who are your customers?
<--- Score

148. What are the success criteria that will indicate that CCNP objectives have been met and the benefits delivered?

<--- Score

149. What CCNP skills are most important?
<--- Score

150. Who uses your product in ways you never expected?
<--- Score

151. What would you recommend your friend do if he/she were facing this dilemma?
<--- Score

152. What is the range of capabilities?
<--- Score

153. Is your strategy driving your strategy? Or is the way in which you allocate resources driving your strategy?
<--- Score

154. Who will be responsible for deciding whether CCNP goes ahead or not after the initial investigations?
<--- Score

155. What did you miss in the interview for the worst hire you ever made?
<--- Score

156. When a packet is denied by an IPv6 traffic filter, which additional action does the device perform?
<--- Score

157. In retrospect, of the projects that you pulled the

plug on, what percent do you wish had been allowed to keep going, and what percent do you wish had ended earlier?

<--- Score

158. How do you go about securing CCNP?

<--- Score

159. How does CCNP integrate with other stakeholder initiatives?

<--- Score

160. What should be alleviated first as a factor for troubleshooting?

<--- Score

161. Do you have the right people on the bus?

<--- Score

162. Do you know who is a friend or a foe?

<--- Score

163. What goals did you miss?

<--- Score

164. Which functions and people interact with the supplier and or customer?

<--- Score

165. Who will determine interim and final deadlines?

<--- Score

166. How do you listen to customers to obtain actionable information?

<--- Score

167. Do CCNP rules make a reasonable demand on a users capabilities?
<--- Score

168. What are the gaps in your knowledge and experience?
<--- Score

169. What is cloud and what are the cloud service models?
<--- Score

170. What should you stop doing?
<--- Score

171. If you had to leave your organization for a year and the only communication you could have with employees/colleagues was a single paragraph, what would you write?
<--- Score

172. What is effective CCNP?
<--- Score

173. Is it economical; do you have the time and money?
<--- Score

174. What are you challenging?
<--- Score

175. Do you think you know, or do you know you know ?
<--- Score

176. Who is the main stakeholder, with ultimate

responsibility for driving CCNP forward?
<--- Score

177. Should all networks have a distinct redundant core layer?
<--- Score

178. At what moment would you think; Will I get fired?
<--- Score

179. What may be the consequences for the performance of an organization if all stakeholders are not consulted regarding CCNP?
<--- Score

180. What counts that you are not counting?
<--- Score

181. Will there be any necessary staff changes (redundancies or new hires)?
<--- Score

182. Are you changing as fast as the world around you?
<--- Score

183. Do you say no to customers for no reason?
<--- Score

184. Which can be used to retrieve a network device configuration?
<--- Score

185. Is there any reason to believe the opposite of my current belief?
<--- Score

186. What would have to be true for the option on the table to be the best possible choice?
<--- Score

187. Do you feel that more should be done in the CCNP area?
<--- Score

188. Why are networks designed with layers?
<--- Score

189. What have you done to protect your business from competitive encroachment?
<--- Score

190. Would you rather sell to knowledgeable and informed customers or to uninformed customers?
<--- Score

191. Who will be the architects of the networked economy?
<--- Score

192. Did your employees make progress today?
<--- Score

193. How likely is it that a customer would recommend your company to a friend or colleague?
<--- Score

194. What is the purpose of CCNP in relation to the mission?
<--- Score

195. Is maximizing CCNP protection the same as

minimizing CCNP loss?
<--- Score

196. What is the overall talent health of your organization as a whole at senior levels, and for each organization reporting to a member of the Senior Leadership Team?
<--- Score

197. How is implementation research currently incorporated into each of your goals?
<--- Score

198. What stupid rule would you most like to kill?
<--- Score

199. If you got fired and a new hire took your place, what would she do different?
<--- Score

200. Whom among your colleagues do you trust, and for what?
<--- Score

201. Is CCNP dependent on the successful delivery of a current project?
<--- Score

202. How do you assess the CCNP pitfalls that are inherent in implementing it?
<--- Score

203. What is your BATNA (best alternative to a negotiated agreement)?
<--- Score

204. How do you set CCNP stretch targets and how do you get people to not only participate in setting these stretch targets but also that they strive to achieve these?

<--- Score

205. What is the source of the strategies for CCNP strengthening and reform?

<--- Score

206. Which models, tools and techniques are necessary?

<--- Score

207. Has implementation been effective in reaching specified objectives so far?

<--- Score

208. Why not do CCNP?

<--- Score

209. What management system can you use to leverage the CCNP experience, ideas, and concerns of the people closest to the work to be done?

<--- Score

210. What is an unauthorized commitment?

<--- Score

211. Are there any activities that you can take off your to do list?

<--- Score

212. Why should you adopt a CCNP framework?

<--- Score

213. What are you trying to prove to yourself, and how might it be hijacking your life and business success?
<--- Score

214. What happens if you do not have enough funding?
<--- Score

215. Think of your CCNP project, what are the main functions?
<--- Score

216. How important is CCNP to the user organizations mission?
<--- Score

217. What will be the consequences to the stakeholder (financial, reputation etc) if CCNP does not go ahead or fails to deliver the objectives?
<--- Score

218. What one word do you want to own in the minds of your customers, employees, and partners?
<--- Score

219. Is a CCNP team work effort in place?
<--- Score

220. What potential megatrends could make your business model obsolete?
<--- Score

221. What is your CCNP strategy?
<--- Score

222. What are the usability implications of CCNP

actions?

<--- Score

223. How are current food safety laws enforced?

<--- Score

224. Why will customers want to buy your organizations products/services?

<--- Score

225. Is your basic point _____ or _____?

<--- Score

226. Is there any existing CCNP governance structure?

<--- Score

Add up total points for this section:
_____ = Total points for this section

Divided by: _____ (number of statements answered) = _____
Average score for this section

Transfer your score to the CCNP Index at the beginning of the Self-Assessment.

CCNP and Managing Projects, Criteria for Project Managers:

1.0 Initiating Process Group: CCNP

1. How well did the chosen processes fit the needs of the CCNP project?

2. How will it affect me?

3. What technical work to do in each phase?

4. Will the CCNP project meet the client requirements, and will it achieve the business success criteria that justified doing the CCNP project in the first place?

5. At which cmmi level are software processes documented, standardized, and integrated into a standard to-be practiced process for your organization?

6. What were the challenges that you encountered during the execution of a previous CCNP project that you would not want to repeat?

7. Were escalated issues resolved promptly?

8. Which of six sigmas dmaic phases focuses on the measurement of internal process that affect factors that are critical to quality?

9. How will you do it?

10. Are you just doing busywork to pass the time?

11. What will you do to minimize the impact should a risk event occur?

12. During which stage of Risk planning are risks prioritized based on probability and impact?

13. Who is involved in each phase?

14. Did the CCNP project team have the right skills?

15. When must it be done?

16. Were decisions made in a timely manner?

17. How is each deliverable reviewed, verified, and validated?

18. Measurable - are the targets measurable?

19. How well did the chosen processes produce the expected results?

20. For technology CCNP projects only: Are all production support stakeholders (Business unit, technical support, & user) prepared for implementation with appropriate contingency plans?

1.1 Project Charter: CCNP

21. Why have you chosen the aim you have set forth?

22. Why do you need to manage scope?

23. How will you learn more about the process or system you are trying to improve?

24. What are the known stakeholder requirements?

25. When do you use a CCNP project Charter?

26. What is the justification?

27. What outcome, in measureable terms, are you hoping to accomplish?

28. What changes can you make to improve?

29. Where and how does the team fit within your organization structure?

30. What are you striving to accomplish (measurable goal(s))?

31. Who is the CCNP project Manager?

32. What date will the task finish?

33. CCNP project objective statement: what must the CCNP project do?

34. Assumptions: what factors, for planning purposes,

are you considering to be true?

35. When is a charter needed?

36. Is it an improvement over existing products?

37. What are the deliverables?

38. What material?

39. How high should you set your goals?

40. What goes into your CCNP project Charter?

1.2 Stakeholder Register: CCNP

41. Who is managing stakeholder engagement?

42. Is your organization ready for change?

43. Who are the stakeholders?

44. How much influence do they have on the CCNP project?

45. What is the power of the stakeholder?

46. What opportunities exist to provide communications?

47. What & Why?

48. How should employers make voices heard?

49. Who wants to talk about Security?

50. How big is the gap?

51. What are the major CCNP project milestones requiring communications or providing communications opportunities?

52. How will reports be created?

1.3 Stakeholder Analysis Matrix: CCNP

53. What do you Evaluate?

54. What organizational arrangements are planned to ensure the CCNP project achieves its social development outcomes?

55. How do they affect the CCNP project and its outcomes?

56. What is your organizations competitors doing?

57. What could your organization improve?

58. Tactics: eg, surprise, major contracts?

59. How do customers express needs?

60. Insurmountable weaknesses?

61. Geographical, export, import?

62. Who has control over whom?

63. Innovative aspects?

64. What coalitions might build around the issues being tackled?

65. Why involve the stakeholder?

66. Organizational Applicability?

67. Why do you care?

68. Competitor intentions - various?

69. Are the interests in line with the program objectives?

70. New markets, vertical, horizontal?

71. Will the impacts be local, national or international?

72. Accreditations, etc?

2.0 Planning Process Group: CCNP

73. Mitigate. what will you do to minimize the impact should a risk event occur?

74. What should you do next?

75. What makes your CCNP project successful?

76. If you are late, will anybody notice?

77. Is the schedule for the set products being met?

78. What good practices or successful experiences or transferable examples have been identified?

79. When will the CCNP project be done?

80. What is a Software Development Life Cycle (SDLC)?

81. How can you tell when you are done?

82. In what way has the CCNP project come up with innovative measures for problem-solving?

83. Have operating capacities been created and/or reinforced in partners?

84. To what extent do the intervention objectives and strategies of the CCNP project respond to your organizations plans?

85. The CCNP project charter is created in which CCNP project management process group?

86. How well defined and documented are the CCNP project management processes you chose to use?

87. What types of differentiated effects are resulting from the CCNP project and to what extent?

88. How does activity resource estimation affect activity duration estimation?

89. If action is called for, what form should it take?

90. To what extent has the intervention strategy been adapted to the areas of intervention in which it is being implemented?

91. Who are the CCNP project stakeholders?

92. Does it make any difference if you are successful?

2.1 Project Management Plan: CCNP

93. Do there need to be organizational changes?

94. Was the peer (technical) review of the cost estimates duly coordinated with the cost estimate center of expertise and addressed in the review documentation and certification?

95. What should you drop in order to add something new?

96. Is there anything you would now do differently on your CCNP project based on past experience?

97. What if, for example, the positive direction and vision of your organization causes expected trends to change resulting in greater need than expected?

98. How do you organize the costs in the CCNP project management plan?

99. Who is the sponsor?

100. If the CCNP project is complex or scope is specialized, do you have appropriate and/or qualified staff available to perform the tasks?

101. Is the budget realistic?

102. When is the CCNP project management plan created?

103. What did not work so well?

104. Are there any client staffing expectations?

105. Has the selected plan been formulated using cost effectiveness and incremental analysis techniques?

106. What is CCNP project scope management?

107. How well are you able to manage your risk?

108. Is the engineering content at a feasibility level-of-detail, and is it sufficiently complete, to provide an adequate basis for the baseline cost estimate?

109. Is there an incremental analysis/cost effectiveness analysis of proposed mitigation features based on an approved method and using an accepted model?

2.2 Scope Management Plan: CCNP

110. Have all documents been archived in a CCNP project repository for each release?

111. Is the CCNP project sponsor clearly communicating the business case or rationale for why this CCNP project is needed?

112. Is your organization structure for both tracking & controlling the budget well defined and assigned to a specific individual?

113. Is the assigned CCNP project manager a PMP (Certified CCNP project manager) and experienced?

114. Does the detailed work plan match the complexity of tasks with the capabilities of personnel?

115. Is there a formal set of procedures supporting Stakeholder Management?

116. Is there a Steering Committee in place?

117. Are vendor contract reports, reviews and visits conducted periodically?

118. Have the personnel with the necessary skills and competence been identified and has agreement for participation in the CCNP project been reached with the appropriate management?

119. Are metrics used to evaluate and manage Vendors?

120. Are staffing resource estimates sufficiently detailed and documented for use in planning and tracking the CCNP project?

121. What are the risks of not having good inter-organization cooperation on the CCNP project?

122. Are meeting objectives identified for each meeting?

123. Are changes in deliverable commitments agreed to by all affected groups & individuals?

124. Are CCNP project contact logs kept up to date?

125. What are the Quality Assurance overheads?

126. Do you have the reasons why the changes to your organizational systems and capabilities are required?

127. Will your organizations estimating methodology be used and followed?

128. Have external dependencies been captured in the schedule?

129. Does all CCNP project documentation reside in a common repository for easy access?

2.3 Requirements Management Plan: CCNP

130. Will the CCNP project requirements become approved in writing?

131. Is the user satisfied?

132. Who has the authority to reject CCNP project requirements?

133. To see if a requirement statement is sufficiently well-defined, read it from the developers perspective. Mentally add the phrase, call me when youre done to the end of the requirement and see if that makes you nervous. In other words, would you need additional clarification from the author to understand the requirement well enough to design and implement it?

134. What cost metrics will be used?

135. Who will approve the requirements (and if multiple approvers, in what order)?

136. How detailed should the CCNP project get?

137. Did you get proper approvals?

138. How will you develop the schedule of requirements activities?

139. When and how will a requirements baseline be established in this CCNP project?

140. What are you trying to do?

141. Are all the stakeholders ready for the transition into the user community?

142. Did you use declarative statements?

143. Is the change control process documented?

144. Which hardware or software, related to, or as outcome of the CCNP project is new to your organization?

145. Who will do the reporting and to whom will reports be delivered?

146. How often will the reporting occur?

147. Will you document changes to requirements?

148. If it exists, where is it housed?

149. What information regarding the CCNP project requirements will be reported?

2.4 Requirements Documentation: CCNP

150. Has requirements gathering uncovered information that would necessitate changes?

151. How linear / iterative is your Requirements Gathering process (or will it be)?

152. Basic work/business process; high-level, what is being touched?

153. Are there any requirements conflicts?

154. Who provides requirements?

155. What is your Elevator Speech?

156. How will requirements be documented and who signs off on them?

157. Do your constraints stand?

158. How does the proposed CCNP project contribute to the overall objectives of your organization?

159. What kind of entity is a problem ?

160. Does the system provide the functions which best support the customers needs?

161. Consistency. are there any requirements conflicts?

162. How do you get the user to tell you what they want?

163. What is effective documentation?

164. How to document system requirements?

165. What can tools do for us?

166. How much does requirements engineering cost?

167. Have the benefits identified with the system being identified clearly?

168. What is a show stopper in the requirements?

169. How do you know when a Requirement is accurate enough?

2.5 Requirements Traceability Matrix: CCNP

170. How small is small enough?

171. Why do you manage scope?

172. How do you manage scope?

173. Do you have a clear understanding of all subcontracts in place?

174. How will it affect the stakeholders personally in career?

175. Will you use a Requirements Traceability Matrix?

176. Why use a WBS?

177. What percentage of CCNP projects are producing traceability matrices between requirements and other work products?

178. Describe the process for approving requirements so they can be added to the traceability matrix and CCNP project work can be performed. Will the CCNP project requirements become approved in writing?

179. What are the chronologies, contingencies, consequences, criteria?

180. What is the WBS?

181. Is there a requirements traceability process in place?

2.6 Project Scope Statement: CCNP

182. If the scope changes, what will the impact be to your CCNP project in terms of duration, cost, quality, or any other important areas of the CCNP project?

183. Is your organization structure appropriate for the CCNP projects size and complexity?

184. Has the CCNP project scope statement been reviewed as part of the baseline process?

185. Will there be a Change Control Process in place?

186. Who will you recommend approve the change, and when do you recommend the change reviews occur?

187. Risks?

188. Once its defined, what is the stability of the CCNP project scope?

189. What process would you recommend for creating the CCNP project scope statement?

190. Which risks does the CCNP project focus on?

191. If there is an independent oversight contractor, have they signed off on the CCNP project Plan?

192. Change management vs. change leadership - what is the difference?

193. If you were to write a list of what should not be included in the scope statement, what are the things that you would recommend be described as out-of-scope?

194. Elements of scope management that deal with concept development ?

195. Are there completion/verification criteria defined for each task producing an output?

196. What went wrong?

197. CCNP project lead, team lead, solution architect?

198. Do you anticipate new stakeholders joining the CCNP project over time?

199. Is there a Quality Assurance Plan documented and filed?

2.7 Assumption and Constraint Log: CCNP

200. What if failure during recovery?

201. Does a documented CCNP project organizational policy & plan (i.e. governance model) exist?

202. Are you meeting your customers expectations consistently?

203. Is the process working, and people are not executing in compliance of the process?

204. Is there adequate stakeholder participation for the vetting of requirements definition, changes and management?

205. Security analysis has access to information that is sanitized?

206. How can you prevent/fix violations?

207. Is the steering committee active in CCNP project oversight?

208. Are there nonconformance issues?

209. Have you eliminated all duplicative tasks or manual efforts, where appropriate?

210. Are there processes in place to ensure internal consistency between the source code components?

211. Should factors be unpredictable over time?

212. Is staff trained on the software technologies that are being used on the CCNP project?

213. Have all necessary approvals been obtained?

214. If it is out of compliance, should the process be amended or should the Plan be amended?

215. Does the CCNP project have a formal CCNP project Plan?

216. Has the approach and development strategy of the CCNP project been defined, documented and accepted by the appropriate stakeholders?

217. What worked well?

218. Are there processes in place to ensure that all the terms and code concepts have been documented consistently?

219. Are funding and staffing resource estimates sufficiently detailed and documented for use in planning and tracking the CCNP project?

2.8 Work Breakdown Structure: CCNP

220. When do you stop?

221. What is the probability of completing the CCNP project in less that xx days?

222. How many levels?

223. Is it still viable?

224. When would you develop a Work Breakdown Structure?

225. How much detail?

226. Can you make it?

227. Is the work breakdown structure (wbs) defined and is the scope of the CCNP project clear with assigned deliverable owners?

228. When does it have to be done?

229. What is the probability that the CCNP project duration will exceed xx weeks?

230. Do you need another level?

231. Who has to do it?

232. How big is a work-package?

233. What has to be done?

234. Where does it take place?

235. Why is it useful?

2.9 WBS Dictionary: CCNP

236. Contemplated overhead expenditure for each period based on the best information currently available?

237. Are overhead cost budgets established for each organization which has authority to incur overhead costs?

238. Are the latest revised estimates of costs at completion compared with the established budgets at appropriate levels and causes of variances identified?

239. Are work packages reasonably short in time duration or do they have adequate objective indicators/milestones to minimize subjectivity of the in process work evaluation?

240. Are overhead costs budgets established on a basis consistent with anticipated direct business base?

241. Are the responsibilities and authorities of each of the above organizational elements or managers clearly defined?

242. What is the goal?

243. Does the contractor require sufficient detailed planning of control accounts to constrain the application of budget initially allocated for future effort to current effort?

244. Should you include sub-activities?

245. Are the variances between budgeted and actual indirect costs identified and analyzed at the level of assigned responsibility for control (indirect pool, department, etc.)?

246. Does the contractors system provide unit or lot costs when applicable?

247. Is future work which cannot be planned in detail subdivided to the extent practicable for budgeting and scheduling purposes?

248. Does the contractors system provide unit costs, equivalent unit or lot costs in terms of labor, material, other direct, and indirect costs?

249. Are data elements summarized through the functional organizational structure for progressively higher levels of management?

250. Are detailed work packages planned as far in advance as practicable?

251. Does the contractors system description or procedures require that the performance measurement baseline plus management reserve equal the contract budget base?

252. Is authorization of budgets in excess of the contract budget base controlled formally and done with the full knowledge and recognition of the procuring activity?

253. Where learning is used in developing underlying budgets is there a direct relationship between anticipated learning and time phased budgets?

254. Is the work done on a work package level as described in the WBS dictionary?

2.10 Schedule Management Plan: CCNP

255. Is a pmo (CCNP project management office) in place and provide oversight to the CCNP project?

256. Is the critical path valid?

257. What threats might prevent you from getting there?

258. Are risk oriented checklists used during risk identification?

259. Alignment to strategic goals & objectives?

260. Will the tools selected accomplish the scheduling needs?

261. Perform reality checks on schedules – are all tasks included?

262. Does the schedule have reasonable float?

263. Do CCNP project teams & team members report on status / activities / progress?

264. Are risk triggers captured?

265. Can additional resources be added to subsequent tasks to reduce the durations of the already stated tasks?

266. Were stakeholders aware and supportive of the principles and practices of modern software estimation?

267. How are CCNP projects different from operations?

268. Has process improvement efforts been completed before requirements efforts begin?

269. Are there checklists created to determine if all quality processes are followed?

270. Are adequate resources provided for the quality assurance function?

271. Identify the amount of schedule variation that triggers a warning. What happens if a warning is triggered?

272. Why conduct schedule analysis?

273. Does all CCNP project documentation reside in a common repository for easy access?

2.11 Activity List: CCNP

274. Can you determine the activity that must finish, before this activity can start?

275. Is there anything planned that does not need to be here?

276. How can the CCNP project be displayed graphically to better visualize the activities?

277. How will it be performed?

278. What went right?

279. Where will it be performed?

280. What is the total time required to complete the CCNP project if no delays occur?

281. In what sequence?

282. What will be performed?

283. How should ongoing costs be monitored to try to keep the CCNP project within budget?

284. What are the critical bottleneck activities?

285. For other activities, how much delay can be tolerated?

286. Is infrastructure setup part of your CCNP project?

287. How do you determine the late start (LS) for each activity?

288. What did not go as well?

289. What is the LF and LS for each activity?

290. How difficult will it be to do specific activities on this CCNP project?

291. What is your organizations history in doing similar activities?

2.12 Activity Attributes: CCNP

292. How else could the items be grouped?

293. Activity: what is In the Bag?

294. Do you feel very comfortable with your prediction?

295. How many resources do you need to complete the work scope within a limit of X number of days?

296. How difficult will it be to complete specific activities on this CCNP project?

297. Does your organization of the data change its meaning?

298. How difficult will it be to do specific activities on this CCNP project?

299. Activity: what is Missing?

300. Resources to accomplish the work?

301. Why?

302. Resource is assigned to?

303. Can you re-assign any activities to another resource to resolve an over-allocation?

304. What activity do you think you should spend the most time on?

305. Activity: fair or not fair?

306. How do you manage time?

307. What is the general pattern here?

308. Are the required resources available or need to be acquired?

309. Would you consider either of corresponding activities an outlier?

2.13 Milestone List: CCNP

310. What is the market for your technology, product or service?

311. When will the CCNP project be complete?

312. How late can the activity finish?

313. Gaps in capabilities?

314. Reliability of data, plan predictability?

315. Sustainable financial backing?

316. Level of the Innovation?

317. What specific improvements did you make to the CCNP project proposal since the previous time?

318. Which path is the critical path?

319. Environmental effects?

320. Milestone pages should display the UserID of the person who added the milestone. Does a report or query exist that provides this audit information?

321. How late can the activity start?

322. How will the milestone be verified?

323. Loss of key staff?

324. Obstacles faced?

325. Describe the industry you are in and the market growth opportunities. What is the market for your technology, product or service?

326. Identify critical paths (one or more) and which activities are on the critical path?

327. Marketing - reach, distribution, awareness?

2.14 Network Diagram: CCNP

328. How confident can you be in your milestone dates and the delivery date?

329. What to do and When?

330. What job or jobs precede it?

331. If a current contract exists, can you provide the vendor name, contract start, and contract expiration date?

332. What are the Key Success Factors?

333. What controls the start and finish of a job?

334. What are the tools?

335. What is the lowest cost to complete this CCNP project in xx weeks?

336. What are the Major Administrative Issues?

337. How difficult will it be to do specific activities on this CCNP project?

338. What activities must occur simultaneously with this activity?

339. Are you on time?

340. What is the completion time?

341. Will crashing x weeks return more in benefits than it costs?

342. Where do you schedule uncertainty time?

343. Which type of network diagram allows you to depict four types of dependencies?

344. Planning: who, how long, what to do?

345. Where do schedules come from?

346. What must be completed before an activity can be started?

2.15 Activity Resource Requirements: CCNP

347. Do you use tools like decomposition and rolling-wave planning to produce the activity list and other outputs?

348. What is the Work Plan Standard?

349. Anything else?

350. Why do you do that?

351. Are there unresolved issues that need to be addressed?

352. Time for overtime?

353. When does monitoring begin?

354. What are constraints that you might find during the Human Resource Planning process?

355. How many signatures do you require on a check and does this match what is in your policy and procedures?

356. How do you handle petty cash?

357. Other support in specific areas?

358. Which logical relationship does the PDM use most often?

2.16 Resource Breakdown Structure: CCNP

359. Which resources should be in the resource pool?

360. Who delivers the information?

361. How should the information be delivered?

362. What defines a successful CCNP project?

363. Why do you do it?

364. Any changes from stakeholders?

365. Who will be used as a CCNP project team member?

366. What is the primary purpose of the human resource plan?

367. Goals for the CCNP project. What is each stakeholders desired outcome for the CCNP project?

368. What is the number one predictor of a groups productivity?

369. Who is allowed to see what data about which resources?

370. What is CCNP project communication management?

371. Is predictive resource analysis being done?

372. Who will use the system?

373. How can this help you with team building?

374. What defines a successful CCNP project?

2.17 Activity Duration Estimates: CCNP

375. Who will provide training for the new application?

376. Is corrective action taken to bring CCNP project performance into line with the CCNP project plan?

377. Why time management?

378. Which is the BEST thing to do to try to complete a CCNP project two days earlier?

379. Are procurement documents used to solicit accurate and complete proposals from prospective sellers?

380. Why do you need a good WBS to use CCNP project management software?

381. Do stakeholders follow a procedure for formally accepting the CCNP project scope?

382. Is action taken to increase the effectiveness and efficiency of CCNP projects?

383. What are two suggestions for ensuring adequate change control on CCNP projects that involve outside contracts?

384. Do procedures exist that identify when and how human resources are introduced and removed from

the CCNP project?

385. Do they make sense?

386. Is a CCNP project charter created once a CCNP project is formally recognized?

387. What do you think the real problem was in this case?

388. If you plan to take the PMP exam soon, what should you do to prepare?

389. Are inspections completed to determine if the results comply with the requirements?

390. Is a standard form used to obtain bids and proposals from prospective sellers?

391. CCNP project manager is using weighted average duration estimates to perform schedule network analysis. Which type of mathematical analysis is being used?

392. Who will promote it?

393. Are CCNP project costs tracked in the general ledger?

394. Are resource rates available to calculate CCNP project costs?

2.18 Duration Estimating Worksheet: CCNP

395. What work will be included in the CCNP project?

396. Science = process: remember the scientific method?

397. What utility impacts are there?

398. Why estimate costs?

399. Will the CCNP project collaborate with the local community and leverage resources?

400. What is the total time required to complete the CCNP project if no delays occur?

401. How should ongoing costs be monitored to try to keep the CCNP project within budget?

402. When does your organization expect to be able to complete it?

403. Can the CCNP project be constructed as planned?

404. Small or large CCNP project?

405. Value pocket identification & quantification what are value pockets?

406. Done before proceeding with this activity or

what can be done concurrently?

407. When, then?

408. How can the CCNP project be displayed graphically to better visualize the activities?

409. What is next?

2.19 Project Schedule: CCNP

410. Why do you think schedule issues often cause the most conflicts on CCNP projects?

411. Should you have a test for each code module?

412. How does a CCNP project get to be a year late ?

413. CCNP project work estimates Who is managing the work estimate quality of work tasks in the CCNP project schedule?

414. How can slack be negative?

415. To what degree is do you feel the entire team was committed to the CCNP project schedule?

416. The wbs is developed as part of a joint planning session. and how do you know that youhave done this right?

417. Verify that the update is accurate. Are all remaining durations correct?

418. How closely did the initial CCNP project Schedule compare with the actual schedule?

419. Are activities connected because logic dictates the order in which others occur?

420. How detailed should a CCNP project get?

421. If you can not fix it, how do you do it differently?

422. Have all CCNP project delays been adequately accounted for, communicated to all stakeholders and adjustments made in overall CCNP project schedule?

423. Why is software CCNP project disaster so common?

424. Your CCNP project management plan results in a CCNP project schedule that is too long. If the CCNP project network diagram cannot change and you have extra personnel resources, what is the BEST thing to do?

425. What is the difference?

426. Did the final product meet or exceed user expectations?

427. Month CCNP project take?

428. Meet requirements?

2.20 Cost Management Plan: CCNP

429. Are cause and effect determined for risks when others occur?

430. Is there anything unique in this CCNP projects scope statement that will affect resources?

431. Are quality inspections and review activities listed in the CCNP project schedule(s)?

432. Was the scope definition used in task sequencing?

433. Is there a formal process for updating the CCNP project baseline?

434. Are the appropriate IT resources adequate to meet planned commitments?

435. Were CCNP project team members involved in the development of activity & task decomposition?

436. Is your organization certified as a supplier, wholesaler, regular dealer, or manufacturer of corresponding products/supplies?

437. What weaknesses do you have?

438. Does the CCNP project have a Quality Culture?

439. Environmental management – what changes in statutory environmental compliance requirements are anticipated during the CCNP project?

440. Has your organization readiness assessment been conducted?

441. Is the CCNP project sponsor clearly communicating the business case or rationale for why this CCNP project is needed?

442. Risk Analysis?

443. Have CCNP project management standards and procedures been identified / established and documented?

444. Forecasts – how will the cost to complete the CCNP project be forecast?

445. Have lessons learned been conducted after each CCNP project release?

2.21 Activity Cost Estimates: CCNP

446. Would you hire them again?

447. What were things that you did well, and could improve, and how?

448. How many activities should you have?

449. Can you delete activities or make them inactive?

450. How do you do activity recasts?

451. Does the activity serve a common type of customer?

452. How do you treat administrative costs in the activity inventory?

453. What is included in indirect cost being allocated?

454. The impact and what actions were taken?

455. In which phase of the acquisition process cycle does source qualifications reside?

456. Why do you manage cost?

457. What is the activity inventory?

458. Who determines when the contractor is paid?

459. Performance bond should always provide what part of the contract value?

460. Will you need to provide essential services information about activities?

461. How do you change activities?

462. Does the estimator estimate by task or by person?

463. What makes a good activity description?

2.22 Cost Estimating Worksheet: CCNP

464. Ask: are others positioned to know, are others credible, and will others cooperate?

465. What happens to any remaining funds not used?

466. What costs are to be estimated?

467. Is the CCNP project responsive to community need?

468. Who is best positioned to know and assist in identifying corresponding factors?

469. What is the estimated labor cost today based upon this information?

470. Does the CCNP project provide innovative ways for stakeholders to overcome obstacles or deliver better outcomes?

471. How will the results be shared and to whom?

472. What info is needed?

473. What can be included?

474. Is it feasible to establish a control group arrangement?

475. Will the CCNP project collaborate with the local

community and leverage resources?

476. What will others want?

477. Can a trend be established from historical performance data on the selected measure and are the criteria for using trend analysis or forecasting methods met?

478. Identify the timeframe necessary to monitor progress and collect data to determine how the selected measure has changed?

479. What additional CCNP project(s) could be initiated as a result of this CCNP project?

480. What is the purpose of estimating?

2.23 Cost Baseline: CCNP

481. Are procedures defined by which the cost baseline may be changed?

482. Does a process exist for establishing a cost baseline to measure CCNP project performance?

483. On time?

484. How difficult will it be to do specific tasks on the CCNP project?

485. Have all approved changes to the schedule baseline been identified and impact on the CCNP project documented?

486. Vac -variance at completion, how much over/ under budget do you expect to be?

487. Have the actual milestone completion dates been compared to the approved schedule?

488. What is the consequence?

489. On budget?

490. How likely is it to go wrong?

491. Have the lessons learned been filed with the CCNP project Management Office?

492. Is there anything you need from upper management in order to be successful?

493. How long are you willing to wait before you find out were late?

494. Are you meeting with your team regularly?

495. Does it impact schedule, cost, quality?

496. Review your risk triggers -have your risks changed?

497. Are there contingencies or conditions related to the acceptance?

2.24 Quality Management Plan: CCNP

498. Who else should be involved ?

499. What has the QM Collaboration done?

500. Who gets results of work?

501. Is this process still needed?

502. What other teams / processes would be impacted by changes to the current process, and how?

503. Contradictory information between different documents?

504. Would impacts defined serve as impediments?

505. What are the appropriate test methods to be used?

506. Can it be done better?

507. How effectively was the Quality Management Plan applied during CCNP project Execution?

508. How is staff informed of proper reporting methods?

509. How do you manage quality?

510. List your organizations customer contact standards that employees are expected to maintain. How are corresponding standards measured?

511. How is staff trained?

512. What else should you do now?

513. Are there unnecessary steps that are creating bottlenecks and/or causing people to wait?

514. When reporting to different audiences, do you vary the form or type of report?

515. What would you gain if you spent time working to improve this process?

516. What is the Difference Between a QMP and QAPP?

517. Does a documented CCNP project organizational policy & plan (i.e. governance model) exist?

2.25 Quality Metrics: CCNP

518. When is the security analysis testing complete?

519. Did the team meet the CCNP project success criteria documented in the Quality Metrics Matrix?

520. Who is willing to lead?

521. What happens if you get an abnormal result?

522. Were quality attributes reported?

523. Are quality metrics defined?

524. What method of measurement do you use?

525. What metrics do you measure?

526. How exactly do you define when differences exist?

527. What level of statistical confidence do you use?

528. How do you calculate such metrics?

529. How effective are your security tests?

530. Which are the right metrics to use?

531. What forces exist that would cause them to change?

532. Are there already quality metrics available that

detect nonlinear embeddings and trends similar to the users perception?

533. Product Availability ?

534. How do you measure?

535. What is the benchmark?

536. What documentation is required?

537. Is quality culture a competitive advantage?

2.26 Process Improvement Plan: CCNP

538. What personnel are the coaches for your initiative?

539. Does your process ensure quality?

540. Who should prepare the process improvement action plan?

541. Are there forms and procedures to collect and record the data?

542. What is the return on investment?

543. What makes people good SPI coaches?

544. Where do you want to be?

545. What personnel are the sponsors for that initiative?

546. Has the time line required to move measurement results from the points of collection to databases or users been established?

547. Are you making progress on your improvement plan?

548. Management commitment at all levels?

549. Are you making progress on the improvement framework?

550. To elicit goal statements, do you ask a question such as, What do you want to achieve?

551. Are you making progress on the goals?

552. Why quality management?

553. What lessons have you learned so far?

554. Everyone agrees on what process improvement is, right?

2.27 Responsibility Assignment Matrix: CCNP

555. Does each role with Accountable responsibility have the authority within your organization to make the required decisions?

556. What expertise is available in your department?

557. How cost benefit analysis?

558. Are too many reports done in writing instead of verbally?

559. The staff characteristics – is the group or the person capable to work together as a team?

560. What are the assigned resources?

561. Are authorized changes being incorporated in a timely manner?

562. Do all the identified groups or people really need to be consulted?

563. What cost control tool do many experts say is crucial to CCNP project management?

564. Do you need to convince people that its well worth the time and effort?

565. Past experience – the person or the group worked at something similar in the past?

566. Which CCNP project management knowledge area is least mature?

567. Are meaningful indicators identified for use in measuring the status of cost and schedule performance?

568. Is the anticipated (firm and potential) business base CCNP projected in a rational, consistent manner?

569. Does the contractor use objective results, design reviews and tests to trace schedule performance?

570. Evaluate the impact of schedule changes, work around, etc?

571. What travel needed?

572. Budgeted cost for work performed?

2.28 Roles and Responsibilities: CCNP

573. What should you do now to ensure that you are exceeding expectations and excelling in your current position?

574. What should you do now to ensure that you are meeting all expectations of your current position?

575. What are your major roles and responsibilities in the area of performance measurement and assessment?

576. Who is involved?

577. To decide whether to use a quality measurement, ask how will you know when it is achieved?

578. Concern: where are you limited or have no authority, where you can not influence?

579. Are your budgets supportive of a culture of quality data?

580. How is your work-life balance?

581. What expectations were met?

582. Do you take the time to clearly define roles and responsibilities on CCNP project tasks?

583. What should you do now to prepare for your career 5+ years from now?

584. What should you highlight for improvement?

585. Do the values and practices inherent in the culture of your organization foster or hinder the process?

586. How well did the CCNP project Team understand the expectations of specific roles and responsibilities?

587. Are your policies supportive of a culture of quality data?

588. Are governance roles and responsibilities documented?

589. Are CCNP project team roles and responsibilities identified and documented?

590. Are the quality assurance functions and related roles and responsibilities clearly defined?

2.29 Human Resource Management Plan: CCNP

591. Is your organization human?

592. What were things that you did very well and want to do the same again on the next CCNP project?

593. How are you going to ensure that you have a well motivated workforce?

594. Are milestone deliverables effectively tracked and compared to CCNP project plan?

595. Is it standard practice to formally commit stakeholders to the CCNP project via agreements?

596. Has the CCNP project scope been baselined?

597. Are updated CCNP project time & resource estimates reasonable based on the current CCNP project stage?

598. Are internal CCNP project status meetings held at reasonable intervals?

599. Were the budget estimates reasonable?

600. Has a resource management plan been created?

601. Was the CCNP project schedule reviewed by all stakeholders and formally accepted?

602. Are people being developed to meet the challenges of the future?

603. Are software metrics formally captured, analyzed and used as a basis for other CCNP project estimates?

604. Is there an on-going process in place to monitor CCNP project risks?

605. Has the scope management document been updated and distributed to help prevent scope creep?

606. Are quality inspections and review activities listed in the CCNP project schedule(s)?

607. Were stakeholders aware and supportive of the principles and practices of modern cost estimation?

2.30 Communications Management Plan: CCNP

608. How is this initiative related to other portfolios, programs, or CCNP projects?

609. Is there an important stakeholder who is actively opposed and will not receive messages?

610. Who were proponents/opponents?

611. Timing: when do the effects of the communication take place?

612. In your work, how much time is spent on stakeholder identification?

613. What steps can you take for a positive relationship?

614. What to know?

615. Are you constantly rushing from meeting to meeting?

616. Do you feel a register helps?

617. How do you manage communications?

618. Who are the members of the governing body?

619. Who is involved as you identify stakeholders?

620. What is the stakeholders level of authority?

621. Do you then often overlook a key stakeholder or stakeholder group?

622. What help do you and your team need from the stakeholder?

623. Which stakeholders are thought leaders, influences, or early adopters?

624. How did the term stakeholder originate?

625. Conflict resolution -which method when?

2.31 Risk Management Plan: CCNP

626. Are status updates being made on schedule and are the updates clearly described?

627. Monitoring -what factors can you track that will enable you to determine if the risk is becoming more or less likely?

628. Who/what can assist?

629. Minimize cost and financial risk?

630. Degree of confidence in estimated size estimate?

631. What risks are tracked?

632. Was an original risk assessment/risk management plan completed?

633. Is the necessary data being captured and is it complete and accurate?

634. Workarounds are determined during which step of risk management?

635. Market risk: will the new product be useful to your organization or marketable to others?

636. Should the risk be taken at all?

637. Mitigation -how can you avoid the risk?

638. Maximize short-term return on investment?

639. Risk may be made during which step of risk management?

640. How risk averse are you?

641. What is the probability the risk avoidance strategy will be successful?

642. Is the process being followed?

643. Do the requirements require the creation of components that are unlike anything your organization has previously built?

644. Risk categories: what are the main categories of risks that should be addressed on this CCNP project?

2.32 Risk Register: CCNP

645. What would the impact to the CCNP project objectives be should the risk arise?

646. Assume the event happens, what is the Most Likely impact?

647. User involvement: do you have the right users?

648. Cost/benefit – how much will the proposed mitigations cost and how does this cost compare with the potential cost of the risk event/situation should it occur?

649. What should you do when?

650. Have other controls and solutions been implemented in other services which could be applied as an alternative to additional funding?

651. Are implemented controls working as others should?

652. Risk probability and impact: how will the probabilities and impacts of risk items be assessed?

653. Risk documentation: what reporting formats and processes will be used for risk management activities?

654. When is it going to be done?

655. Why would you develop a risk register?

656. What is the appropriate level of risk management for this CCNP project?

657. What could prevent you delivering on the strategic program objectives and what is being done to mitigate corresponding issues?

658. When will it happen?

659. Financial risk -can your organization afford to undertake the CCNP project?

660. What action, if any, has been taken to respond to the risk?

661. Who is going to do it?

662. How often will the Risk Management Plan and Risk Register be formally reviewed, and by whom?

663. Severity Prediction?

664. Are corrective measures implemented as planned?

2.33 Probability and Impact Assessment: CCNP

665. How much risk do others need to take?

666. Do you have specific methods that you use for each phase of the process?

667. How would you assess the risk management process in the CCNP project?

668. What is the probability of the risk occurring?

669. Can you stabilize dynamic risk factors?

670. Do you manage the process through use of metrics?

671. How do you define a risk?

672. Which role do you have in the CCNP project?

673. Can the CCNP project proceed without assuming the risk?

674. Do you have a consistent repeatable process that is actually used?

675. My CCNP project leader has suddenly left your organization, what do you do?

676. Is it necessary to deeply assess all CCNP project risks?

677. Who has experience with this?

678. Are end-users enthusiastically committed to the CCNP project and the system/product to be built?

679. Are people attending meetings and doing work?

680. Do requirements demand the use of new analysis, design, or testing methods?

681. What will be the likely political environment during the life of the CCNP project?

682. What would be the effect of slippage?

683. Will there be an increase in the political conservatism?

684. Have decisions that should be left open because of inadequate information on technology been identified and responsibility assigned for reducing the uncertainty?

2.34 Probability and Impact Matrix: CCNP

685. What are the chances the risk events will occur?

686. What is the political situation at present?

687. How should you structure risks?

688. Are staff committed for the duration of the CCNP project?

689. What is the risk appetite?

690. Are enough people available?

691. Does the customer understand the software process?

692. How much is the probability of the risk occurring?

693. Is the present organizational structure for handling the CCNP project sufficient?

694. Have top software and customer managers formally committed to support the CCNP project?

695. Are CCNP project requirements stable?

696. Can it be changed quickly?

697. Prioritized components/features?

698. Are you working on the right risks?

699. Which is the BEST thing to do?

700. Can you avoid altogether some things that might go wrong?

701. How solid is the CCNP projection of competitive reaction?

702. Is the delay in one subCCNP project going to affect another?

703. What needs to be DONE?

2.35 Risk Data Sheet: CCNP

704. What is the chance that it will happen?

705. What are you weak at and therefore need to do better?

706. What is the likelihood of it happening?

707. If it happens, what are the consequences?

708. What actions can be taken to eliminate or remove risk?

709. How reliable is the data source?

710. Potential for recurrence?

711. What can happen?

712. How can it happen?

713. What were the Causes that contributed?

714. What was measured?

715. Is the data sufficiently specified in terms of the type of failure being analyzed, and its frequency or probability?

716. What are your core values?

717. What will be the consequences if the risk happens?

718. Whom do you serve (customers)?

719. What are you trying to achieve (Objectives)?

720. What will be the consequences if it happens?

2.36 Procurement Management Plan: CCNP

721. Does the CCNP project have a formal CCNP project Charter?

722. Is the CCNP project sponsor clearly communicating the business case or rationale for why this CCNP project is needed?

723. Have adequate resources been provided by management to ensure CCNP project success?

724. Staffing Requirements?

725. Have lessons learned been conducted after each CCNP project release?

726. Are the schedule estimates reasonable given the CCNP project?

727. Similar CCNP projects?

728. Has the schedule been baselined?

729. Is it standard practice to formally commit stakeholders to the CCNP project via agreements?

730. Is there a procurement management plan in place?

731. What are your quality assurance overheads?

732. Is there a Quality Management Plan?

733. How will the duration of the CCNP project influence your decisions?

734. Is an industry recognized mechanized support tool(s) being used for CCNP project scheduling & tracking?

2.37 Source Selection Criteria: CCNP

735. Will the technical evaluation factor unnecessarily force the acquisition into a higher-priced market segment?

736. Do you have a plan to document consensus results including disposition of any disagreement by individual evaluators?

737. Do you consider all weaknesses, significant weaknesses, and deficiencies?

738. What documentation is needed for a tradeoff decision?

739. Do you prepare an independent cost estimate?

740. Comparison of each offers prices to the estimated prices -are there significant differences?

741. What are the special considerations for preaward debriefings?

742. When is it appropriate to issue a DRFP?

743. What are the guidelines regarding award without considerations?

744. When is it appropriate to issue a Draft Request for Proposal (DRFP)?

745. What should communications be used to accomplish?

746. How do you ensure an integrated assessment of proposals?

747. Does an evaluation need to include the identification of strengths and weaknesses?

748. What information is to be provided and when should it be provided?

749. Is there collaboration among your evaluators?

750. What should a DRFP include?

751. How are clarifications and communications appropriately used?

752. Is a cost realism analysis used?

753. How should the preproposal conference be conducted?

2.38 Stakeholder Management Plan: CCNP

754. Where are the verification requirements to be documented (eg purchase order, agreement etc)?

755. Are assumptions being identified, recorded, analyzed, qualified and closed?

756. Have key stakeholders been identified?

757. Does the CCNP project have a formal CCNP project Plan?

758. Is the quality assurance team identified?

759. When would you develop a CCNP project Execution Plan?

760. Are best practices and metrics employed to identify issues, progress, performance, etc.?

761. How, to whom and how frequently will Risk status be reported?

762. What process was used to identify risks to the CCNP projects success?

763. Was trending evident between audits?

764. Have activity relationships and interdependencies within tasks been adequately identified?

765. Is an industry recognized mechanized support tool(s) being used for CCNP project scheduling & tracking?

766. Who is responsible for accepting the reports produced by the process?

767. What potential impact does the stakeholder have on the CCNP project?

768. Are the CCNP project plans updated on a frequent basis?

769. Have all stakeholders been identified?

770. Are regulatory inspections considered part of quality control?

771. Does the business case include how the CCNP project aligns with your organizations strategic goals & objectives?

772. Who might be involved in developing a charter?

773. What information should be collected?

2.39 Change Management Plan: CCNP

774. Is there support for this application(s) and are the details available for distribution?

775. What goal(s) do you hope to accomplish?

776. Clearly articulate the overall business benefits of the CCNP project -why are you doing this now?

777. How prevalent is Resistance to Change?

778. When developing your communication plan do you address : When should the given message be communicated?

779. How will the stakeholders share information and transfer knowledge?

780. Do there need to be new channels developed?

781. What risks may occur upfront?

782. What work practices will be affected?

783. Impact of systems implementation on organization change?

784. Who will do the training?

785. Has a training need analysis been carried out?

786. Is there a software application relevant to this deliverable?

787. What are the major changes to processes?

788. Where will the funds come from?

789. How much CCNP project management is needed?

790. Who is responsible for which tasks?

791. What relationships will change?

792. Do you need new systems?

3.0 Executing Process Group: CCNP

793. How could you control progress of your CCNP project?

794. Will new hardware or software be required for servers or client machines?

795. What type of people would you want on your team?

796. What are deliverables of your CCNP project?

797. Who will be the main sponsor?

798. Do CCNP project managers understand your organizational context for CCNP projects?

799. Does the case present a realistic scenario?

800. Why should CCNP project managers strive to make jobs look easy?

801. How does the job market and current state of the economy affect human resource management?

802. What were things that you need to improve?

803. Is the CCNP project making progress in helping to achieve the set results?

804. What is the critical path for this CCNP project and how long is it?

805. Does the CCNP project team have the right skills?

806. How is CCNP project performance information created and distributed?

807. Would you rate yourself as being risk-averse, risk-neutral, or risk-seeking?

808. Who will provide training?

809. What are the typical CCNP project management skills?

810. Do your results resemble a normal distribution?

3.1 Team Member Status Report: CCNP

811. When a teams productivity and success depend on collaboration and the efficient flow of information, what generally fails them?

812. Is there evidence that staff is taking a more professional approach toward management of your organizations CCNP projects?

813. What is to be done?

814. How can you make it practical?

815. How does this product, good, or service meet the needs of the CCNP project and your organization as a whole?

816. What specific interest groups do you have in place?

817. The problem with Reward & Recognition Programs is that the truly deserving people all too often get left out. How can you make it practical?

818. Will the staff do training or is that done by a third party?

819. Are your organizations CCNP projects more successful over time?

820. Does every department have to have a CCNP

project Manager on staff?

821. Are the products of your organizations CCNP projects meeting customers objectives?

822. Does your organization have the means (staff, money, contract, etc.) to produce or to acquire the product, good, or service?

823. Are the attitudes of staff regarding CCNP project work improving?

824. How much risk is involved?

825. Does the product, good, or service already exist within your organization?

826. Do you have an Enterprise CCNP project Management Office (EPMO)?

827. How will resource planning be done?

828. How it is to be done?

829. Why is it to be done?

3.2 Change Request: CCNP

830. Screen shots or attachments included in a Change Request?

831. What are the basic mechanics of the Change Advisory Board (CAB)?

832. Who is responsible for the implementation and monitoring of all measures?

833. How to get changes (code) out in a timely manner?

834. Should staff call into the helpdesk or go to the website?

835. What is the relationship between requirements attributes and reliability?

836. What is a Change Request Form?

837. Are there requirements attributes that are strongly related to the occurrence of defects and failures?

838. Have all related configuration items been properly updated?

839. Why do you want to have a change control system?

840. Who needs to approve change requests?

841. Who is included in the change control team?

842. Since there are no change requests in your CCNP project at this point, what must you have before you begin?

843. What mechanism is used to appraise others of changes that are made?

844. How are changes requested (forms, method of communication)?

845. Can you answer what happened, who did it, when did it happen, and what else will be affected?

846. For which areas does this operating procedure apply?

847. What should be regulated in a change control operating instruction?

848. Have scm procedures for noting the change, recording it, and reporting it been followed?

849. What are the requirements for urgent changes?

3.3 Change Log: CCNP

850. Do the described changes impact on the integrity or security of the system?

851. Does the suggested change request seem to represent a necessary enhancement to the product?

852. Should a more thorough impact analysis be conducted?

853. Does the suggested change request represent a desired enhancement to the products functionality?

854. How does this change affect scope?

855. Is the change request within CCNP project scope?

856. How does this relate to the standards developed for specific business processes?

857. How does this change affect the timeline of the schedule?

858. Is the change request open, closed or pending?

859. Is the change backward compatible without limitations?

860. Is this a mandatory replacement?

861. Will the CCNP project fail if the change request is not executed?

862. Is the submitted change a new change or a modification of a previously approved change?

863. When was the request submitted?

864. When was the request approved?

865. Is the requested change request a result of changes in other CCNP project(s)?

866. Where do changes come from?

867. Who initiated the change request?

3.4 Decision Log: CCNP

868. How does provision of information, both in terms of content and presentation, influence acceptance of alternative strategies?

869. Meeting purpose; why does this team meet?

870. What is the average size of your matters in an applicable measurement?

871. How does the use a Decision Support System influence the strategies/tactics or costs?

872. It becomes critical to track and periodically revisit both operational effectiveness; Are you noticing all that you need to, and are you interpreting what you see effectively?

873. Linked to original objective?

874. Is everything working as expected?

875. What was the rationale for the decision?

876. How consolidated and comprehensive a story can you tell by capturing currently available incident data in a central location and through a log of key decisions during an incident?

877. What is your overall strategy for quality control / quality assurance procedures?

878. Behaviors; what are guidelines that the team has

identified that will assist them with getting the most out of team meetings?

879. Do strategies and tactics aimed at less than full control reduce the costs of management or simply shift the cost burden?

880. Who is the decisionmaker?

881. Decision-making process; how will the team make decisions?

882. Who will be given a copy of this document and where will it be kept?

883. How effective is maintaining the log at facilitating organizational learning?

884. How does an increasing emphasis on cost containment influence the strategies and tactics used?

885. Adversarial environment. is your opponent open to a non-traditional workflow, or will it likely challenge anything you do?

886. Is your opponent open to a non-traditional workflow, or will it likely challenge anything you do?

887. What are the cost implications?

3.5 Quality Audit: CCNP

888. Does the supplier use a formal quality system?

889. How does your organization know that the quality of its supervisors is appropriately effective and constructive?

890. How does your organization know that its Strategic Plan is providing the best guidance for the future of your organization?

891. How does your organization know that its planning processes are appropriately effective and constructive?

892. How does your organization know that its staff have appropriate access to a fair and effective grievance process?

893. How does your organization know that its relationships with the community at large are appropriately effective and constructive?

894. Are all areas associated with the storage and reconditioning of devices clean, free of rubbish, adequately ventilated and in good repair?

895. How does your organization know whether they are adhering to mission and achieving objectives?

896. How does your organization know that its security arrangements are appropriately effective and constructive?

897. How does your organization know that its system for inducting new staff to maximize workplace contributions are appropriately effective and constructive?

898. How does your organization know that its system for recruiting the best staff possible are appropriately effective and constructive?

899. How does your organization know that its management of its ethical responsibilities is appropriately effective and constructive?

900. Is your organizational structure established and each positions responsibility defined?

901. Are the intentions consistent with external obligations (such as applicable laws)?

902. Statements of intent remain exactly that until they are put into effect. The next step is to deploy the already stated intentions. In other words, do the plans happen in reality?

903. Is quality audit a prerequisite for program accreditation or program recognition?

904. Have the risks associated with the intentions been identified, analyzed and appropriate responses developed?

905. How does your organization know that its public relations and marketing systems are appropriately effective and constructive?

906. How does your organization know that its system for ensuring that its training activities are appropriately resourced and support is appropriately effective and constructive?

907. How does your organization know that its staff placements are appropriately effective and constructive in relation to program-related learning outcomes?

3.6 Team Directory: CCNP

908. What are you going to deliver or accomplish?

909. Who are the Team Members?

910. How do unidentified risks impact the outcome of the CCNP project?

911. Process decisions: do invoice amounts match accepted work in place?

912. Days from the time the issue is identified?

913. Decisions: what could be done better to improve the quality of the constructed product?

914. Who will write the meeting minutes and distribute?

915. How does the team resolve conflicts and ensure tasks are completed?

916. Have you decided when to celebrate the CCNP projects completion date?

917. Does a CCNP project team directory list all resources assigned to the CCNP project?

918. Process decisions: are all start-up, turn over and close out requirements of the contract satisfied?

919. How and in what format should information be presented?

920. Process decisions: is work progressing on schedule and per contract requirements?

921. Where will the product be used and/or delivered or built when appropriate?

922. Decisions: is the most suitable form of contract being used?

923. Process decisions: are contractors adequately prosecuting the work?

924. How will you accomplish and manage the objectives?

925. Process decisions: are there any statutory or regulatory issues relevant to the timely execution of work?

926. When will you produce deliverables?

927. What needs to be communicated?

3.7 Team Operating Agreement: CCNP

928. Do you begin with a question to engage everyone?

929. Must your team members rely on the expertise of other members to complete tasks?

930. Do you prevent individuals from dominating the meeting?

931. What went well?

932. What is teaming?

933. Did you draft the meeting agenda?

934. Are there more than two functional areas represented by your team?

935. Must your members collaborate successfully to complete CCNP projects?

936. Is compensation based on team and individual performance?

937. Do you vary your voice pace, tone and pitch to engage participants and gain involvement?

938. What is the number of cases currently teamed?

939. Methodologies: how will key team processes be implemented, such as training, research, work deliverable production, review and approval

processes, knowledge management, and meeting procedures?

940. Communication protocols: how will the team communicate?

941. What are the current caseload numbers in the unit?

942. Are there influences outside the team that may affect performance, and if so, have you identified and addressed them?

943. Do team members need to frequently communicate as a full group to make timely decisions?

944. Did you recap the meeting purpose, time, and expectations?

945. What types of accommodations will be formulated and put in place for sustaining the team?

946. Do you leverage technology engagement tools group chat, polls, screen sharing, etc.?

947. Seconds for members to respond?

3.8 Team Performance Assessment: CCNP

948. To what degree are the members clear on what they are individually responsible for and what they are jointly responsible for?

949. To what degree will the team adopt a concrete, clearly understood, and agreed-upon approach that will result in achievement of the teams goals?

950. To what degree are the goals realistic?

951. How does CCNP project termination impact CCNP project team members?

952. To what degree do team members frequently explore the teams purpose and its implications?

953. To what degree are staff involved as partners in the improvement process?

954. What are teams?

955. To what degree do the goals specify concrete team work products?

956. If you are worried about method variance before you collect data, what sort of design elements might you include to reduce or eliminate the threat of method variance?

957. Is there a particular method of data analysis that

you would recommend as a means of demonstrating that method variance is not of great concern for a given dataset?

958. How do you recognize and praise members for contributions?

959. To what degree can the team ensure that all members are individually and jointly accountable for the teams purpose, goals, approach, and work-products?

960. How hard do you try to make a good selection?

961. To what degree can all members engage in open and interactive considerations?

962. To what degree does the teams work approach provide opportunity for members to engage in results-based evaluation?

963. To what degree are the teams goals and objectives clear, simple, and measurable?

964. Individual task proficiency and team process behavior: what is important for team functioning?

965. What is method variance?

966. To what degree does the teams approach to its work allow for modification and improvement over time?

967. To what degree will the team ensure that all members equitably share the work essential to the success of the team?

3.9 Team Member Performance Assessment: CCNP

968. What stakeholders must be involved in the development and oversight of the performance plan?

969. What is collaboration?

970. How accurately is your plan implemented?

971. How is performance assessment used in making future award decisions including options and extend/compete decisions?

972. What are best practices for delivering and developing training evaluations to maximize the benefits of leveraging emerging technologies?

973. How do you use data to inform instruction and improve staff achievement?

974. How do you create a self-sustaining capacity for a collaborative culture?

975. In what areas would you like to concentrate your knowledge and resources?

976. How is assessment information achieved, stored?

977. What are top priorities?

978. Is there reluctance to join a team?

979. To what degree are the skill areas critical to team performance present?

980. What is needed for effective data teams?

981. To what degree does the teams purpose contain themes that are particularly meaningful and memorable?

982. Should a ratee get a copy of all the raters documents about the employees performance?

983. How are training activities developed from a technical perspective?

984. How do you currently account for your results in the teams achievement?

985. What evaluation results do you have?

986. What is a general description of the processes under performance measurement and assessment?

987. How do you start collaborating?

3.10 Issue Log: CCNP

988. How much time does it take to do it?

989. Who needs to know and how much?

990. Which team member will work with each stakeholder?

991. How do you manage human resources?

992. What is the impact on the risks?

993. Who is the issue assigned to?

994. Persistence; will users learn a work around or will they be bothered every time?

995. Who reported the issue?

996. Do you have members of your team responsible for certain stakeholders?

997. What does the stakeholder need from the team?

998. Which stakeholders can influence others?

999. Why multiple evaluators?

1000. Who have you worked with in past, similar initiatives?

1001. Are stakeholder roles recognized by your organization?

1002. Is access to the Issue Log controlled?

4.0 Monitoring and Controlling Process Group: CCNP

1003. Is progress on outcomes due to your program?

1004. Just how important is your work to the overall success of the CCNP project?

1005. Do clients benefit (change) from the services?

1006. Specific - is the objective clear in terms of what, how, when, and where the situation will be changed?

1007. Feasibility: how much money, time, and effort can you put into this?

1008. Who are the CCNP project stakeholders?

1009. Did it work?

1010. Is there undesirable impact on staff or resources?

1011. How well defined and documented were the CCNP project management processes you chose to use?

1012. Is there adequate validation on required fields?

1013. Based on your CCNP project communication management plan, what worked well?

1014. User: who wants the information and what are

they interested in?

1015. What were things that you did very well and want to do the same again on the next CCNP project?

1016. How are you doing?

1017. How is agile CCNP project management done?

1018. Do the partners have sufficient financial capacity to keep up the benefits produced by the programme?

1019. Contingency planning. if a risk event occurs, what will you do?

1020. Where is the Risk in the CCNP project?

4.1 Project Performance Report: CCNP

1021. To what degree are the goals ambitious?

1022. To what degree does the information network provide individuals with the information they require?

1023. What is the degree to which rules govern information exchange between individuals within your organization?

1024. To what degree are the structures of the formal organization consistent with the behaviors in the informal organization?

1025. To what degree does the formal organization make use of individual resources and meet individual needs?

1026. To what degree can team members vigorously define the teams purpose in considerations with others who are not part of the functioning team?

1027. To what degree are the demands of the task compatible with and converge with the mission and functions of the formal organization?

1028. To what degree can team members frequently and easily communicate with one another?

1029. To what degree will the approach capitalize on and enhance the skills of all team members in a manner that takes into consideration other demands on members of the team?

1030. To what degree can the team measure progress against specific goals?

1031. To what degree will team members, individually and collectively, commit time to help themselves and others learn and develop skills?

1032. To what degree are the tasks requirements reflected in the flow and storage of information?

1033. To what degree does the teams work approach provide opportunity for members to engage in open interaction?

1034. To what degree are sub-teams possible or necessary?

1035. To what degree will new and supplemental skills be introduced as the need is recognized?

1036. To what degree can the cognitive capacity of individuals accommodate the flow of information?

4.2 Variance Analysis: CCNP

1037. What causes selling price variance?

1038. Are the bases and rates for allocating costs from each indirect pool consistently applied?

1039. How does the monthly budget compare to the actual experience?

1040. What are the actual costs to date?

1041. Are data elements reconcilable between internal summary reports and reports forwarded to the stakeholders?

1042. When, during the last four quarters, did a primary business event occur causing a fluctuation?

1043. Are all cwbs elements specified for external reporting?

1044. Are overhead costs budgets established on a basis consistent with the anticipated direct business base?

1045. What does a favorable labor efficiency variance mean?

1046. The anticipated business volume?

1047. Why are standard cost systems used?

1048. Is all contract work included in the CWBS?

1049. Does the contractors system identify work accomplishment against the schedule plan?

1050. Can the contractor substantiate work package and planning package budgets?

1051. What is the expected future profitability of each customer?

1052. Who are responsible for overhead performance control of related costs?

1053. What is the budgeted cost for work scheduled?

1054. Are overhead cost budgets established for each department which has authority to incur overhead costs?

1055. What is the actual cost of work performed?

1056. What types of services and expense are shared between business segments?

4.3 Earned Value Status: CCNP

1057. What is the unit of forecast value?

1058. Where are your problem areas?

1059. How much is it going to cost by the finish?

1060. Are you hitting your CCNP projects targets?

1061. Where is evidence-based earned value in your organization reported?

1062. Verification is a process of ensuring that the developed system satisfies the stakeholders agreements and specifications; Are you building the product right? What do you verify?

1063. How does this compare with other CCNP projects?

1064. When is it going to finish?

1065. Earned value can be used in almost any CCNP project situation and in almost any CCNP project environment. it may be used on large CCNP projects, medium sized CCNP projects, tiny CCNP projects (in cut-down form), complex and simple CCNP projects and in any market sector. some people, of course, know all about earned value, they have used it for years - but perhaps not as effectively as they could have?

1066. Validation is a process of ensuring that

the developed system will actually achieve the stakeholders desired outcomes; Are you building the right product? What do you validate?

1067. If earned value management (EVM) is so good in determining the true status of a CCNP project and CCNP project its completion, why is it that hardly any one uses it in information systems related CCNP projects?

4.4 Risk Audit: CCNP

1068. What responsibilities for quality, errors, and outcomes have been delegated to staff (or others) without adequate oversight?

1069. Are team members trained in the use of the tools?

1070. Does your organization communicate regularly and effectively with its members?

1071. Tradeoff: how much risk can be tolerated and still deliver the products where they need to be?

1072. Have you considered the health and safety of everyone in your organization and do you meet work health and safety regulations?

1073. Are all participants informed of safety issues?

1074. Are tool mentors available?

1075. Does your organization have a register of insurance policies detailing all current insurance policies?

1076. What are the boundaries of the auditors responsibility for policing management fidelity?

1077. Are contracts reviewed before renewal?

1078. What expertise do auditors need to generate effective business-level risk assessments, and to what extent do auditors currently possess the already stated attributes?

1079. Is your organization able to present documentary evidence in support of compliance?

1080. Do you ensure the recommended rules of play and protocols are followed for your activity?

1081. Are all programs planned and conducted according to recognized safety standards?

1082. Does your organization meet the terms of any contracts with which it is involved?

1083. Is there a screening process that will ensure all participants have the fitness and skills required to safely participate?

1084. Have risks been considered with an insurance broker or provider and suitable insurance cover been arranged?

1085. Does the team have the right mix of skills?

1086. Does the customer understand the process?

1087. Is there (or should there be) some impact on the process of setting materiality when the auditor more effectively identifies higher risk areas of the financial statements?

4.5 Contractor Status Report: CCNP

1088. What are the minimum and optimal bandwidth requirements for the proposed solution?

1089. How is risk transferred?

1090. Describe how often regular updates are made to the proposed solution. Are corresponding regular updates included in the standard maintenance plan?

1091. Who can list a CCNP project as organization experience, your organization or a previous employee of your organization?

1092. What is the average response time for answering a support call?

1093. What was the final actual cost?

1094. What was the actual budget or estimated cost for your organizations services?

1095. How does the proposed individual meet each requirement?

1096. What process manages the contracts?

1097. What was the overall budget or estimated cost?

1098. Are there contractual transfer concerns?

1099. How long have you been using the services?

1100. What was the budget or estimated cost for your organizations services?

1101. If applicable; describe your standard schedule for new software version releases. Are new software version releases included in the standard maintenance plan?

4.6 Formal Acceptance: CCNP

1102. Was the CCNP project work done on time, within budget, and according to specification?

1103. Was business value realized?

1104. Did the CCNP project achieve its MOV?

1105. What was done right?

1106. What features, practices, and processes proved to be strengths or weaknesses?

1107. How well did the team follow the methodology?

1108. Do you perform formal acceptance or burn-in tests?

1109. What can you do better next time?

1110. How does your team plan to obtain formal acceptance on your CCNP project?

1111. What lessons were learned about your CCNP project management methodology?

1112. Was the CCNP project managed well?

1113. What is the Acceptance Management Process?

1114. Was the sponsor/customer satisfied?

1115. Do you buy-in installation services?

1116. Does it do what client said it would?

1117. Who supplies data?

1118. Is formal acceptance of the CCNP project product documented and distributed?

1119. Have all comments been addressed?

1120. General estimate of the costs and times to complete the CCNP project?

1121. What function(s) does it fill or meet?

5.0 Closing Process Group: CCNP

1122. Were the outcomes different from the already stated planned?

1123. What is the CCNP project Management Process?

1124. What were things that you did very well and want to do the same again on the next CCNP project?

1125. How well did you do?

1126. Are there funding or time constraints?

1127. Did you do things well?

1128. What was learned?

1129. Is this a follow-on to a previous CCNP project?

1130. What is the overall risk of the CCNP project to your organization?

1131. If a risk event occurs, what will you do?

1132. Does the close educate others to improve performance?

1133. Who are the CCNP project stakeholders?

1134. What level of risk does the proposed budget represent to the CCNP project?

5.1 Procurement Audit: CCNP

1135. Are there mechanisms for evaluating the departments suppliers performance in relation to prices, quality, delivery and innovation?

1136. Is the accounting distribution of expenses included with the request for payment?

1137. Was the admissibility of variants displayed in the contract notice?

1138. Does the procurement process compile basic procurement information such as how much is bought and spend with individual suppliers?

1139. Were additional deliveries a partial replacement for normal supplies or installations or an extension of existing supplies or installations?

1140. Does the procurement CCNP project have a clear goal and does the goal meet the specified needs of the users?

1141. Months to reflect any changes in policy?

1142. Is the performance of the procurement function/unit regularly evaluated?

1143. Is it assessed whether well-functioning markets exist for the departments services/tasks?

1144. Are the journals and ledgers kept current for all funds?

1145. Is there no evidence of any external or superior pressure to reach a specific result?

1146. When competitive dialogue was used, did the contracting authority provide sufficient justification for the use of this procedure and was the contract actually particularly complex?

1147. Did your organization decide for an appropriate and admissible procurement procedure?

1148. Is your organization transparent about winning bids and prices?

1149. Were any additional works or deliveries admissible, without recourse to a new procurement procedure?

1150. Does your organization have an overall strategy and/or policy on public procurement, providing guidance for procuring entities?

1151. Were the tender documents comprehensive, transparent and free from restrictions or conditions which would discriminate against certain suppliers?

1152. Who is verifying the performance of the contract and approving payments?

1153. Is there no evidence of favouritism towards a particular contractor during the evaluation and negotiation processes?

1154. Are internal control mechanisms performed before payments?

5.2 Contract Close-Out: CCNP

1155. Has each contract been audited to verify acceptance and delivery?

1156. How/when used ?

1157. Was the contract sufficiently clear so as not to result in numerous disputes and misunderstandings?

1158. What happens to the recipient of services?

1159. Was the contract type appropriate?

1160. Change in attitude or behavior?

1161. Have all acceptance criteria been met prior to final payment to contractors?

1162. Change in knowledge?

1163. Have all contracts been completed?

1164. Are the signers the authorized officials?

1165. Parties: Authorized?

1166. Why Outsource?

1167. Was the contract complete without requiring numerous changes and revisions?

1168. Have all contract records been included in the CCNP project archives?

1169. Parties: who is involved?

1170. How does it work?

1171. How is the contracting office notified of the automatic contract close-out?

1172. What is capture management?

1173. Have all contracts been closed?

1174. Change in circumstances?

5.3 Project or Phase Close-Out: CCNP

1175. Was the schedule met?

1176. What was expected from each stakeholder?

1177. Planned remaining costs?

1178. Was the user/client satisfied with the end product?

1179. What is this stakeholder expecting?

1180. What advantages do the an individual interview have over a group meeting, and vice-versa?

1181. What was the preferred delivery mechanism?

1182. What stakeholder group needs, expectations, and interests are being met by the CCNP project?

1183. What are the informational communication needs for each stakeholder?

1184. Is the lesson based on actual CCNP project experience rather than on independent research?

1185. What could be done to improve the process?

1186. Complete yes or no?

1187. What hierarchical authority does the stakeholder have in your organization?

1188. What could have been improved?

1189. Planned completion date?

1190. Were risks identified and mitigated?

1191. Did the delivered product meet the specified requirements and goals of the CCNP project?

5.4 Lessons Learned: CCNP

1192. If you had to do this CCNP project again, what is the one thing that you would change (related to process, not to technical solutions)?

1193. How many government and contractor personnel are authorized for the CCNP project?

1194. Would you spend your own money to fix this issue?

1195. Are corrective actions needed?

1196. What is the economic growth rate?

1197. What is your organizational ideology?

1198. Under what legal authority did your organization head and program manager direct your organization and CCNP project?

1199. Did the CCNP project change significantly?

1200. What are the funding priorities for intelligence?

1201. Was CCNP project performance validated or challenged?

1202. How did the estimated CCNP project Budget compare with the total actual expenditures?

1203. What regulatory regime controlled how your organization head and program manager directed your organization and CCNP project?

1204. How well did the CCNP project Manager respond to questions or comments related to the CCNP project?

1205. What are the skills directly related to the task?

1206. What are the external dependencies?

1207. How smooth do you feel Integration has been?

1208. What on the CCNP project worked well and was effective in the delivery of the product?

1209. How much of your time was spent on other than this CCNP project?

1210. Are there any data that you have overlooked in identifying lessons?

1211. How effectively were issues resolved before escalation was necessary?

Index

270

housed   139
humans   9
hypotheses   57
identified   3, 20, 22, 24, 35, 60-61, 64, 68, 84, 132, 136-137,
141, 150-151, 173, 178, 186-187, 189, 199, 208-209, 221, 223, 225,
228, 255
identifies   244
identify1, 11-12, 17-18, 23, 64-66, 74, 154, 160, 166, 177, 192, 208,
240
ideology   256
ignore 20
ignoring   110
imbedded   88
impact6, 34, 44, 46, 49-50, 54-55, 79, 114, 125-126, 132, 144, 174,
178-179, 187, 196, 198, 200, 209-210, 218, 225, 229, 233, 235, 244
impacted   43, 180
impacts   45, 53, 131, 168, 180, 196
implement   20, 46, 60, 87, 138
implicit110
import 130
important   20, 23, 30, 61-62, 67, 109, 112-113, 115, 122, 144,
192, 230, 235
improve   4, 11, 72-73, 75-79, 81-83, 85, 127, 130, 174, 181,
212, 225, 231, 249, 254
improved   2, 73-74, 86, 88, 255
improving   80, 215
inactive   174
inadequate   1, 199
incentives   89
incident   220
include   80, 151, 207, 209, 229
included   4, 9, 18, 51, 145, 153, 168, 174, 176, 216-217, 239,
245-246, 250, 252
INCLUDES   11
including   32, 34, 48, 97-98, 206, 231
increase   74, 102, 166, 199
increased   109
increasing   103, 221
incurred   53
in-depth   10, 12
indicate   59, 96, 114
indicated   96
indicators   22, 49, 51, 59, 62, 67, 71, 76, 97, 150, 187

members 1, 32, 40, 69, 96, 153, 172, 192, 225, 227-230, 233, 237-238, 243
memorable 232
Mentally 138
mentors 243
message 91, 210
messages 192
method 49, 135, 168, 182, 193, 217, 229-230
methods 30, 41, 44, 67, 103, 177, 180, 198-199
metrics 6, 34, 64, 89, 136, 138, 182, 191, 198, 208
milestone 5, 159, 161, 178, 190
milestones 129, 150
minimize 125, 132, 150, 194
minimizing 69, 120
minimum 245
minority 24
minutes 35, 225
missed 47, 106
missing 68, 109, 157
mission 61, 70, 119, 122, 222, 237
mitigate 77, 132, 197
mitigated 2, 255
Mitigation 135, 194
modeling 64
models 26, 51, 67, 117, 121
modern 154, 191
modified 93
module 170
moment 118
moments 58
momentum 106
Monday 1
monetary 23
monitor 89, 91, 95, 177, 191
monitored 88, 90, 155, 168
monitoring 7, 89, 91, 93-94, 96, 163, 194, 216, 235
monthly 239
Months 1, 250
morning 1
motivate 102
motivated 190
motivation 27, 91
moving 113

Printed in Great Britain
by Amazon